es

Swami Bhaskarananda

Life in Indian Monasteries

Reminiscences about Monks of the Ramakrishna Order

by Swami Bhaskarananda

Viveka Press

Seattle

Viveka Press, Seattle 98102

©2004 by The Vedanta Society of Western Washington

For more information write to:
Viveka Press
2716 Broadway Avenue East
Seattle, WA 98102-3909 USA
Phone: (206) 323-1228
Email: vivekapress@vedanta-seattle.org
http://www.vedanta-seattle.org/

Published 2004
Printed in Canada

Publisher's Cataloging-in-Publication
(Provided by Quality Books Inc)

Bhaskarananda, Swami.
    Life in Indian monasteries : reminiscences about
monks of the Ramakrishna Order / by Swami Bhaskarananda
    p. cm.
    Includes bibliographical references and index.
    LCCN 2003096154
    ISBN 1-884852-06-8

    1. Ramakrishna Order--History--Anecdotes.
2. Ramakrishna Order--Biography--Anecdotes.
3. Monasteries, Hindu--India--Ancedotes. 4. Monastic and
religious life (Hinduism)--India--Anecdotes.
I. Title

BL1280.273.B43 2004   294.5'55
                             QBI03-200730

About the Cover: A painting by Richard Engstrom of the Sri Ramakrishna Temple at Belur Math, the Headquarters of the Ramakrishna Order in India.

THE HOLY MOTHER SRI SARADA DEVI
(1853–1920)

Humbly dedicated to the Holy Mother Sri Sarada Devi
whose grace, love and compassion have always been
protecting the monks of the Ramakrishna Order

Contents

Preface

During one of my visits to India a brother monk said to me, "Several books have been written about the first generation monks of our Order, but there are very few books about the monks of the second generation. We know that many of them had wonderful, inspirational lives. Once, we, the monks of the third generation who have had the privilege of knowing them are dead and gone, their precious memory will be lost forever. Why don't you write about them?" It is his request that encouraged me to write this book.

I am also aware that most devotees of our Order, particularly those in the West, know very little about the way of life in Indian monasteries. They are naturally curious to know what the monks do in their day-to-day life, how they interact with one another, etc., etc.

To satisfy their curiosity, different aspects of our monastic life have been presented through this book. The book also contains many inspirational anecdotes, numerous photographs of monks, and other details of monastic life, not known to outsiders.

In the publication of this book the following persons have helped immensely and I acknowledge their loving assistance with deep gratitude.

- William Page for his valuable suggestions and help in editing the first manuscript of the book.

- Devra A. Freedman for her help in editing, and preparing the index.

- Richard Engstrom for designing and illustrating the cover.

- Charles Mathias for his illustrations.

- Bhaskar Puri for his illustration.

- Swami Brahmadevananda, Swami Bodhasarananda and Swami Dayarupananda of our Order for their help in procuring some of the photographs and biodata of the swamis mentioned in this book.

- Pradipta Chakraborty for procuring a photograph and additional biodata of Swami Purushatmananda.

- Charles S. Wirth for providing assistance with the typesetting and printing of the manuscript.

- Brahmachari Vijnanachaitanya and Allen Freedman for editing the pictures of some swamis.

- Swami Shantarupananda for his reminiscences of Swami Shantananda.

I shall consider my labor well rewarded if the book proves to be helpful to the readers.

Swami Bhaskarananda

Introduction

Ramdas Kathiababa, the renowned 19th century saint of Vrindaban in India, used to say that it is extremely hard to understand a holy man, because a holy man is like an elephant. An elephant has its tusks, and some inner teeth to chew its food. The tusks are visible to others, but not the inner teeth. Similarly, people see only the outer personality of a holy man, not the inner personality. The holy man behaves with outsiders in a certain way, but he hides his inner personality. That inner personality is his true spiritual personality. This analogy is applicable to the monks of the Ramakrishna Order as well. At this point an uninformed reader may naturally ask, "What's the Ramakrishna Order?"

The Ramakrishna Order is a Hindu monastic order formally founded by Swami Vivekananda in the early part of the 20th century. The swami named the order after his deceased guru, Sri Ramakrishna.

The Ramakrishna Order is like a tree with two trunks originating from its root system. The root system represents the life and teachings of Sri Ramakrishna, the most famous and highly revered spiritual personality of 19th century India. He is also considered a Divine Incarnation by thousands of devotees all over the world today. The two trunks of the Ramakrishna Order are (1) the Ramakrishna Math and (2) the Ramakrishna Mission.

In the *General Report of the Ramakrishna Math and the Ramakrishna Mission,* a concise history of the Ramakrishna Order has been given as follows:

> Born in 1836 in a pious brahmin (priestly) family at Kamarpukur, a remote village of West Bengal, Sri Ramakrishna attained an exalted state

of spiritual illumination that had never before been achieved by any other spiritual genius in India or elsewhere. Shortly after the passing away of this prophet of harmony of religions, in August 1886, a monastic order bearing his name was organized in pursuance of his own instructions, with a monastery (Math) at Baranagore, a northern suburb of Calcutta, by his sannyasin disciples headed by Swami Vivekananda. Gradually it set for itself a twofold ideal: to create a band of sannyasin teachers of Vedanta as propounded by Sri Ramakrishna and practically illustrated by his own life; and in conjunction with the lay disciples to carry on missionary and philanthropic work, looking upon all, irrespective of caste, creed or color, as veritable manifestations of the Divine. For some time the latter work was carried on through an association called the Ramakrishna Mission Association, started by Swami Vivekananda in May 1897, shortly after his return from the West. In 1899 he shifted the Math, which had changed places several times by then, to its present site at Belur, across the river Ganga, about six kilometers north of Howrah railway station, where it set itself more vigorously to the task of training a band of monks inspired with the twin ideals of Self-realization and service to the world. Soon after this the Math authorities took upon themselves the work of the Mission Association.

The Ramakrishna Math was registered as a [religious] trust in 1901. To facilitate the work of the Mission Association and for giving it a legal status, a society named the Ramakrishna Mission was registered in 1909 under Act XXI of 1860. Its management was vested in a Governing Body. Both the Math and the Mission gradually extended their spheres of activity as a result of which a number of branches in different parts of the country (India) and abroad came into existence.

Excluding the headquarters at Belur, on March 31, 2002, the Ramakrishna Mission had 90 centers, while the Ramakrishna Math had 83. Other than India, the Ramakrishna Order (the Ramakrishna Math and the Ramakrishna Mission) had centers in Argentina, Bangladesh, Brazil, Sri Lanka, Mauritius, Fiji, Australia, Singapore, Malaysia, Russia, Japan, the United Kingdom, France, the Netherlands, Switzerland, Canada and the United States of America.

Swami Vivekananda
1863–1902

Other than these centers, there are several hundred centers in India and abroad that are run by devotees and admirers of Sri Ramakrishna. Such centers are usually conducted under the guidance of monks of the Ramakrishna Order, and follow the ideal and pattern of spiritual and philanthropic activities conducted by the Order. Without counting similar centers that are abroad, there were 249 such centers in India run by devotees until 1990. Since then some other new centers also have come into existence.

In the 1950's the Ramakrishna Order also created its women's wing in the form of a twin organization named Sri Sarada Math and Ramakrishna Sarada Mission. After creating this organization, the Ramakrishna Order made it a completely independent and autonomous body to be run entirely by the nuns. This organization, which now has several centers in India and abroad, conducts the same kinds of activities as those of the Ramakrishna Order in India and abroad.

Some characteristics of the Ramakrishna Order:[1]

1. **No miracle-mongering:** Sri Ramakrishna considered the desire for and use of miraculous powers a great obstacle to

---

[1]. Adapted from a talk given by Swami Gahanananda on Dec. 27, 1990, at the conference of Ramakrishna-Vivekananda Peruvai, Tamil Nadu, organized by Sri Ramakrishna Math, Madras, India. Swami Gahanananda is now the senior Vice-President of the Ramakrishna Order.

spiritual progress and discouraged all interest in them. The followers of Sri Ramakrishna are expected to be free from religious hypocrisy and spiritual pretensions.

2. **Modern outlook:** According to the Ramakrishna Order, our way of life, social manners, personal habits, and attitudes should be modern and progressive. Relics of past social customs like caste distinctions have no place in either our individual or collective life.

3. **Non-sectarian approach:** Swami Vivekananda stated that the one thing Sri Ramakrishna never liked was setting limits to God. God has infinite powers and can assume different forms. A true follower of Sri Ramakrishna looks upon all religions as so many valid means of realizing the Ultimate Truth, and regards the different spiritual practices and techniques in the different religions as being suited to the varying temperaments of individuals. Those who belong to the Ramakrishna Order never associate themselves with fanatical religious groups or leaders.

4. **No connection with politics:** Members of the Ramakrishna Order keep away from political parties and ideologies and never get involved in politically contrived controversial situations.

5. **Selfless love:** Sri Ramakrishna was the embodiment of selfless love. This love manifested itself fully through the Holy Mother Sri Sarada Devi[2] and Swami Vivekananda. The selfless love of these great personages is a precious heritage of the Ramakrishna Order. This love, manifested

---

2. The Holy Mother Sri Sarada Devi is the spiritual consort of Sri Ramakrishna. She is also looked upon as a divine incarnation and revered by thousands of people in India as well as abroad.

outwardly as hospitality and concern for the well-being of all, is extended by the various centers and members of the Ramakrishna Order.

6. **Harmony of religions:** Sri Ramakrishna was a prophet of the harmony of religions. According to him, all religions are so many paths to the same Divine Reality. Members of the Ramakrishna Order therefore respect all religions and believe in religious harmony.

Life in the Ramakrishna Order: Readers of this book may naturally be curious about life in the Ramakrishna Order. To satisfy that curiosity, the following passages, with some minor modifications, are quoted from a booklet by Swami Tapasyananda,[3] one of the Ramakrishna Order's past Vice-Presidents.

> In monastic life, as in community life, the individual is participating in the general group consciousness and is therefore propped up or pulled down by that consciousness as the case may be, according to the standard of excellence prevailing in the group. The new self-consciousness of being the member of a group of elite, together with a host of inhibitions like vows, traditions, dress, association and so on, raises a solid barrier of protection behind which even one comparatively weak can operate with sure chances of success, provided one is sincere.

> Bhakti-yoga, Jnana-yoga, Raja-yoga and Karma-yoga (in other words, the path of devotion, the path of philosophical inquiry, the path of meditation, and the path of right action), all form the recognized Sadhanas of the Order. But work has special importance, because according to the rules laid down by Swami Vivekananda, every member, whatever his predilections, must do some work in the service of Sri Ramakrishna. Work cannot therefore be avoided in the name of a pseudo-spirituality, and those who are of that mentality will find themselves misfits in the Order.

3. *For Enquirers About Ramakrishna Math and Ramakrishna Mission* by Swami Tapasyananda. Second revised edition. pp. 46-50. Publishers: Sri Ramakrishna Math, Madras, India.

An organization, like a State, however, requires not only geniuses but also ordinary folks, not only leaders but also followers. In the Order of Sri Ramakrishna all are therefore welcome, talented and highly qualified persons as also those who are not extraordinary, provided that they are attracted by the idea of living a life of renunciation and service. Renunciation implies the eschewal of personal ambitions, family relations, possessions, luxury and sex. An individual can practice renunciation only if the urges mentioned before find fulfillment in the higher satisfaction which devotional life offers.

Service implies the dedication of one's energies and capacities to the works of the Order conceiving it as a symbol of Sri Ramakrishna. Spiritual talents are therefore more important than worldly abilities, but by the very nature and object of the Order a harmonious combination of both is the ideal.

Monastic life, therefore, offers to persons having the required temperament, the best opportunity of developing their capacities and of living their lives in a way that will be of maximum benefit to themselves and the world at large. The conditions of life in the Order are such that any one with the right temperament can easily adjust himself to them.

In the matter of food, clothing and housing, no doubt, simplicity is the rule, but conditions are not prohibitively austere. Middle class standards obtaining in the country are generally observed in these matters in the Math (monastery). Though the monks have no salaries or any other kind of personal income, all their legitimate needs are met by the institution (Order). The monastic vow of poverty therefore does not mean penury and indigence. So also obedience and discipline, while being fundamental in the monastic code of conduct, are not allowed to degenerate into servility and abjectness. While personal ambition has no place, scope for great achievements is open to persons of ability and courage.

Swami Vivekananda lived and preached at a time when India was yet in political bondage. Young men were, therefore, naturally engaged in the struggle for political freedom in the belief that it would solve all our problems. After political independence was attained, we have now come to understand that it has no meaning without economic independence, and the country is, therefore, struggling for that through planning and industrialization. But sooner or later it will be realized that without moral, religious and spiritual freedom—freedom from the animal in man—even economic freedom can offer no solace to the people. It is desirable that at least the more thoughtful sections in the country are prepared to face this disillusionment sufficiently early.

For the attainment of this spiritual freedom the country requires a huge army of workers cast in the mold that Swami Vivekananda has prepared through the harmonious combination of Jnana-yoga, Bhakti-yoga, Raja-yoga, and Karma-yoga. The monastic Order is the great legacy he has left to posterity for accomplishing this purpose. Now that the country is independent, there are no patriotic inhibitions standing in the way of the youth taking to a life of spiritual life and service. It is up to them to respond to the call of Swami Vivekananda, join the Order in large numbers and get their lives molded for special service in India and abroad.

In short, the **ideal** of the Ramakrishna Order is to strive for inner perfection through God-realization and at the same time to work for the good of the world.

The **aim** of the monastic Order is to practice and preach the Eternal Religion (Sanatana Dharma), as embodied in the lives and teachings of Sri Ramakrishna, Sri Sarada Devi, and Swami Vivekananda.

The **motto** of the Ramakrishna Order is Renunciation and Service, and the Harmony of Religions.

The **method** is Work as Worship.

The **activities** of the Order are ritualistic worship, meditation and spiritural instruction; training of monastics; propagation of ethical, spiritual and cultural values through preaching and publication of books and magazines; providing general and technical education built on an ethical and spiritual foundation; running orphanages; medical services; relief and rehabilitation work during natural calamities; integrated rural development and welfare programs; and religio-cultural activities.

Life in Indian Monasteries

*Reminiscences About the Monks
of the First Generation*

⧖ BROTHERLY LOVE

The following incident happened many years ago at the Bhubaneswar ashrama of the Ramakrishna Order in India. At that time Swami Brahmananda, the President of the Ramakrishna Order, was residing there. One day he called Swami Gangeshananda, a junior monk, and said to him, "Bring me some holy Ganga water."

Swami Gangeshananda brought a small bottle of Ganga water to Swami Brahmananda, who sprinkled some of it on his body. Putting the bottle aside, Swami Brahmananda called his *sevak* (attendant), Swami Nirvanananda. When the swami came, Swami Brahmananda pointed to a book in a bookcase, and asked Swami Nirvanananda to bring it to him. Then Swami Brahmananda sat down on a chair, apparently to read it. But he did not open the book. Instead, he looked at it for a while, and then closing his eyes, sat for some time as though meditating. Then he returned the book to Swami Nirvanananda and asked him to put the book back on the shelf. After that Swami Brahmananda got up and walked out of the room.

Swami Gangeshananda watched everything from a distance. He became curious to know why Swami Brahmananda felt he had to purify himself with Ganga water before touching the book. What holy book could it be that needed such purification? To satisfy his curiosity, Swami Gangeshananda took the book from the shelf. To his amazement he saw that it was not a religious book at all; it was a copy of *Emerson's Essays.*

Swami Gangeshananda couldn't at first understand why Swami Brahmananda considered the book so holy. But when he opened the book he saw Swami Vivekananda's handwritten inscription on the first page, indicating that he had given the book to Swami Brahmananda as a loving gift. Swami

SWAMI BRAHMANANDA
(1863–1922)

Gangeshananda now understood that the book was so sacred to Swami Brahmananda because it had come from Swami Vivekananda. According to Sri Ramakrishna, Swami Vivekananda was born a free soul and was the greatest among his disciples. Sri Ramakrishna considered him an incarnation of the ancient sage Nara, as well as of Lord Narayana.

This incident proves what deep respect and admiration Swami Brahmananda, who himself was a great saint, had for his brother disciple Swami Vivekananda. Swami Brahmananda's spiritual emotion was roused thinking of the book's association with Swami Vivekananda.

Part I

I heard this story around 1970 from Swami Gangeshananda when I was staying at Belur Math.[4]

TO GOD-REALIZED SOULS THE WORLD IS DIVINE PLAY

Swami Purushatmananda, more popularly known as Prabuddha Maharaj, came to our Shillong ashrama for a visit. Knowing that he had met some of the great disciples of Sri Ramakrishna, we requested him to tell us about them. Then he told us the following story about Swami Brahmananda:

"I'll tell you an incident about Swami Brahmananda. The first time I visited Belur Math I went to see Swami Brahmananda. I was told that he was then walking on the eastern veranda of the second floor of our original monastery building. When I went there, I couldn't muster enough courage to even salute him, he was so extremely grave. I sat on the cement floor of the veranda at a distance from him. Some other devotees were also seated there. It was early in the morning. Just then a monk came, saluted Swami Brahmananda and said, 'Maharaj, I've got to go to court today in connection with a court case.'

"Hearing that, Swami Brahmananda's mood suddenly changed. Very cheerfully he said to the monk, 'Go ahead. Fight the opposing party using all your strength. How can they win? We are monks; we have no dearth of time. No matter how long it takes to win, we'll go on fighting!' I later heard that the litigation was due to a bad neighbor trying to illegally encroach upon Belur Math property.

---

4. Belur Math means Belur Monastery. Located in Belur, a town about five miles from Calcutta, it is the headquarters of the Ramakrishna Order.

"I had heard that God-realized souls view the world as the sporting ground of God. They find great joy in seeing the Divine play all around them. They see Divinity everywhere. There is nothing good or bad in the games that God plays, because God is beyond good and evil. Spiritually enlightened souls like Swami Brahmananda enjoy seeing the Divine play, and take part in it heartily. In the eyes of Swami Brahmananda, the Belur Math litigation was nothing but another game being played by God. That's why he encouraged the monk to enthusiastically pursue the court case."

⧗ WHO CAN KNOW A KNOWER OF BRAHMAN?

Swami Devananda, a disciple of Swami Brahmananda, told me this story about Swami Turiyananda, one of those exalted saintly disciples of Sri Ramakrishna.

At the time of the story, Swami Turiyananda was staying at the Ramakrishna Mission Sevashrama in Varanasi. This was after his return from America. Swami Devananda (1897–1992), a junior monk, was then staying for a while in the

SWAMI TURIYANANDA
(1863–1922)

Part I

Varanasi sevashrama. He considered himself lucky that his stay there gave him the opportunity to have the holy company of Swami Turiyananda. He would go to his room every day, salute him, and sit there for a while listening to his conversation with the other monks. Every time he entered Swami Turiyananda's room and saluted him, the swami would smile and make kind inquiries of him. And that would fill the heart of Swami Devananda with joy.

Swami Turiyananda's health was not good at that time, and he had to be on a special diet. An attendant swami took care of his food, and would cook dishes suitable for him. One day the attendant swami asked Swami Devananda to help him prepare Swami Turiyananda's food. Swami Devananda was overjoyed at this opportunity to serve Swami Turiyananda. When he went to the small kitchen to help, the attendant swami showed him the mortar and pestle and naming some spices, said to him, "Prepare a paste of each of these spices separately and give them to me."

In his entire life Swami Devananda had never entered a kitchen other than to eat his meals. His family always had had cooks; and like many male members of upper middle class Indian families, he had never learned to cook. Nor had he ever gone to buy groceries. Paid servants did that.

As a result, Swami Devananda had never seen the numerous spices that are used in Indian cooking in their original form, and couldn't recognize them. So he said to the attendant swami, "Please show me what the spices look like, then I'll prepare the pastes."

The attendant swami was surprised at this. He thought that Swami Devananda was giving some lame excuse to avoid helping. He didn't believe Swami Devananda when he had said that he didn't know how to recognize the different spices. We can't blame the attendant swami for this, because very rarely do you find someone who has grown up in India and yet cannot recognize the spices used in everyday cooking. Therefore, with great displeasure he told Swami Devananda, "Go away, I don't need your help!"

The next day, as he normally did, Swami Devananda went to see Swami Turiyananda and saluted him. But Swami Turiyananda turned his face away. He wouldn't even look at Swami Devananda. Nor would he say a single word to him. This behavior continued for three or four days. Swami Devananda was extremely upset about this. He could easily guess that Swami Turiyananda's icy behavior had something to do with what happened between him and the attendant swami over preparing the spice pastes. It was clear that the attendant swami must have complained about him to Swami Turiyananda.

Swami Devananda finally went to Swami Turiyananda, and with tears in his eyes said, "Maharaj (revered sir), you are a knower of Brahman (God); you must know everything. You know that what I told the attendant swami was true. I really cannot recognize the different spices."

Swami Turiyananda said to Swami Devananda, "If you can't recognize spices, how will you recognize God? And who has told you that I'm a knower of Brahman?"

What did Swami Turiyananda mean when he said, "Who has told you that I am a knower of Brahman?" Was he denying that he was a knower of Brahman? Or did he mean that only another knower of Brahman had the right to declare him a knower of Brahman, and not Swami Devananda, who hadn't experienced Brahman yet? I am convinced that the second possibility is correct.

Years before, when Swami Vivekananda first introduced Swami Turiyananda to the American devotees, he said to them, "I'm sending to you one of my brother disciples who is an embodiment of brahmanical virtues. He is an ideal brahmin, a knower of Brahman. Seeing him you will come to know how the highest spirituality can be manifested in human life." Who other than the great Swami Vivekananda was a better connoisseur of the spirituality of Swami Turiyananda, or for that matter of any other saint?

Some other things also need to be explained here. Contrary to the expectation of many, God-realized souls do not try to read other people's thoughts unless they feel divinely inspired to do so. These great souls have a natural tendency to remain immersed in God. To try to know other people's thoughts is usually against their nature. Staunchly established as they are in moral and ethical virtues, entering into other people's private minds is considered highly unethical by them. Due to his young age and inability to understand the behavior of exalted saintly souls, Swami Devananda expected Swami Turiyananda to automatically know his thoughts. But that was a mistake.

Aside from that, one may wonder why a saint like Swami Turiyananda should form an adverse opinion about Swami Devananda just from the words of his attendant. Swami Turiyananda should have asked Swami Devananda about what had happened. And that would have cleared up all misunderstanding. But saintly souls like Swami Turiyananda are established in the practice of truthfulness. As they themselves are truthful they have a natural tendency to trust others. That's why he trusted the words of the attendant swami.

Still a question remains as to why Swami Turiyananda behaved with Swami Devananda so coldly. Why did he stop talking to him? Well, as far as we have come to know from the knowledgeable elders of our Order, saints have various ways of transforming the natures of others that are around them. Sometimes they shower their selfless love on others, sometimes they scold, and sometimes they use cold behavior. Swami Turiyananda decided to cure Swami Devananda's supposed defect of character by being cold to him. It is also possible that Swami Devananda, young as he was, had been getting attached to getting a lot of love and attention from Swami Turiyananda. For a monk such a tendency could be a barrier to loving God wholeheartedly. Swami Turiyananda had come to notice that defect and wanted to help Swami Devananda get rid of his craving for love and attention.

In the later years of his life, Swami Turiyananda suffered from chronic physical ailments that required care from attendant monks. He used to tell them, "You nurse my body, and I nurse your minds." Once without any obvious reason, he suddenly startled a young monk by a severe outburst of scolding. When asked by another monk why he had done that, Swami Turiyananda replied, "I saw a dark cloud of negative thoughts about to enter the mind of that monk. My scolding startled him and helped him to protect himself from those harmful thoughts."

THE IMPORTANCE OF NOT ASKING FOR ANYTHING

I heard this story from Swami Niramayananda (1911-1984), a senior monk of the Ramakrishna Order, while I was in India. He was a disciple of Swami Akhandananda, one of those great saintly disciples of Sri Ramakrishna. Swami Niramayananda's

SWAMI AKHANDANANDA
(1864–1937)

pre-monastic name was Bibhuti. As a *brahmachari* (novice) he was known as Brahmachari Bibhuti. At the time of the incident I am going to narrate, he was staying at our Sargachhi ashrama in Bengal with his guru, Swami Akhandananda.

A junior professor named Madhavrao Golwalkar was teaching in Benares Hindu University in the early 1930s. After teaching at the university for three years, he resigned his position and went to Nagpur. There he studied law and became a lawyer. In Nagpur he came in contact with Swami Bhaskareswarananda, head of the Nagpur branch of the Ramakrishna Order. From him he came to know that one of the disciples of Sri Ramakrishna, Swami Akhandananda, was then living at the Sargachhi ashrama in Bengal. Around that time Golwalkar developed great spiritual yearning and keenly felt the need for a guru. So he went to the Sargachhi ashrama to have spiritual initiation *(diksha)* from the swami. After initiation Golwalkar continued to stay on as a brahmachari for a while.

While at the ashrama, Golwalkar gave personal service of various kinds to his guru with all his heart and soul. He followed his guru like a shadow most of the time, always making himself available to serve.

Once, late at night, Brahmachari Bibhuti heard Swami Akhandananda talking aloud to someone. Bibhuti wondered why the swami was talking so loudly at that hour. Curious, he came to the door of the swami's room and saw an unexpected sight. The door was open and a kerosene lantern was lighting up the room. Swami Akhandananda was seated on his bed, and Golwalkar was kneeling on the floor facing the swami with his hands folded in salutation.

Apparently in response to Golwalkar's prayer, Swami Akhandananda was giving him his blessings. Bibhuti heard the swami say to Golwalkar: "You will have the knowledge of Brahman!"

A few days later, with his guru's permission, Golwalkar left the ashrama. Later in life, he became renowned in India as a leader of a well-known idealistic youth organization.

Witnessing that incident, Bibhuti felt a great sadness of heart, because Swami Akhandananda had never blessed him the way he had blessed Golwalkar. Bibhuti felt convinced that he didn't have much spiritual potential and didn't deserve the blessing of his guru.

As days passed, his sadness deepened. Then one day Swami Akhandananda said to Bibhuti, "I have to go to the bathroom. Please bring a pot of water so that I can rinse my feet after I have used the bathroom." The bathroom was a separate building, away from the residential quarters of the ashrama. It was in a secluded area surrounded by trees. Bibhuti did as he was asked. He walked behind his guru with a pot of water. Swami Akhandananda approached the bathroom, but didn't enter it. He turned around and said to Bibhuti, "Bibhuti, those who pray for something, get it; but those who don't ask for anything get much more." So saying the swami returned to his room.

Bibhuti understood that his guru had come to know the cause of his sadness, even though he hadn't expressed it to him. He also understood that there was selfishness even in asking for blessings in spiritual life. Those who are totally self-less—those who do not ask for anything—they alone get the highest rewards in spiritual life.

⧖ SAINTS ARE NOT IDENTIFIED WITH THEIR BODIES

Once Swami Shivananda, the President of the Ramakrishna Order, was not well. A devotee asked him, "How are you Maharaj?"

Swami Shivananda replied, "My body is not well, but I'm all right."

SWAMI SHIVANANDA
(1854–1934)

Swami Pavanananda, a disciple of Swami Shivananda, told me a story about Swami Shivananda that expresses the same idea more eloquently.

Once Swami Pavanananda came to Belur Math to see Swami Shivananda who was then bedridden with a sudden flare-up of asthma.

Swami Pavanananda entered Swami Shivananda's room, saluted him and then sat quietly on the floor. He was very distressed at the sight of his guru's intense suffering. Swami Shivananda was breathing with great difficulty and coughing frequently. His difficulty in breathing had reddened his fair face. Swami Pavanananda couldn't help thinking, "Besides being a spiritually illumined soul, my guru is also an apostle of Sri Ramakrishna, the Divine Incarnation of this age. Why then should he suffer like this?"

As soon as that thought entered Swami Pavanananda's mind, Swami Shivananda sat up on his bed with a beaming face and smiled at his disciple. All signs of suffering disappeared. Swami Pavanananda was amazed at this wonderful transformation. He realized that Swami Shivananda could at any moment withdraw his mind from his body. Though living in a body, he was completely free from it because he was a *jivanmukta*—one who had attained liberation from the bondage of the body.

SOME REMINISCENCES ABOUT SWAMI VIJNANANANDA

I was talking to Ramji, the chauffeur of the Ramakrishna Mission Tuberculosis Sanatorium in Ranchi. He said, "Maharaj, I've been lucky to have driven many great swamis of the Ramakrishna Mission. I even drove Swami Vijnanananda once."

"Really?" I asked.

Ramji replied, "Yes, it's true. But after driving a few miles, suddenly the engine died. I got out of the stalled car and started repairing the engine. Then Swami Vijnanananda said, 'Ramji, if you have any difficulty, ask me for help. I was once an engineer, you know!'

SWAMI VIJNANANANDA
(1868–1938)

"I said, 'Maharaj, please sit in the car and just bless me, then I'll be able to repair the car.' Luckily I was shortly able to get the car going."

Ramji continued, "I grew up in Varanasi in close association with the monks of the Ramakrishna Mission Sevashrama. The monks loved me very much. As a boy I even played volleyball with them.

"After I became a young man I got my driver's license in Varanasi and began working as a salaried driver. Once, when I was working as the driver of a government officer in Bihar, I received a letter from revered Sailen Maharaj from Allahabad. He was the sevak (attendant) of Swami Vijnanananda at the Allahabad ashrama. He wrote, 'Ramji, this year we are going to observe Durga Puja (worship) in our ashrama. If you come, you can be of great help to us.'

"I talked to my boss and requested a few days' leave during the time of the puja, and he kindly granted my prayer. I thought that I would first go to Varanasi and then to Allahabad. So I boarded a train for Varanasi. On the way the train stopped for a while at a small railroad station. When I looked out the window I saw many lotus flowers in a nearby pond. I immediately got off the train and went to the pond. Meanwhile the train left.

"There was a villager standing close to the pond. I asked him to pluck some lotuses for me. His initial reluctance to respond to my request promptly disappeared when I offered him some money. The man collected a large number of flowers, packed them nicely, and then carried the bundle to the railroad station, where I had to wait for the next train for Varanasi.

"Arriving in Varanasi, I went straight to the Ramakrishna Advaita Ashrama and offered some lotuses for the worship. Then I took a train for Allahabad. When I arrived at the Allahabad Ramakrishna ashrama, revered Sailen Maharaj received me. Seeing all those lotuses, he became extremely happy and went and informed Swami Vijnanananda. When Swami Vijnanananda came out of his room, revered Sailen Maharaj introduced me to him saying, 'Maharaj, this young man's name is Ramji. From a long distance he has brought all these lotuses for the worship of the Divine Mother Durga.'

"Swami Vijnanananda became very pleased to see the flowers. He first looked at the flowers, then at me, and remarked, 'Very *parishkar* (a Bengali word meaning "clean" or "pure").' I felt like he had seen me inside out with his penetrating eyes. This is the first time I saw him, and I was completely overwhelmed by his spiritual presence."

Even though the swami was usually very grave, he could be humorous as well. The following reminiscence will prove this point. A young boy named Dinanath[5] came all the way from

---

5. Later Dinanath joined the Ramakrishna Order and became known as Brahmachari Medhachaitanya.

the county of Midnapore to Belur Math. He came to have diksha (spiritual initiation) from Swami Vijnanananda. Dinanath was of very small stature for his age. When he first went to see Swami Vijnanananda, the swami pointed to a large suitcase in his room and said humorously, "You're so small, I'll put you inside this suitcase!"

Dinanath says, "On the day of my initiation, as instructed earlier, I entered Swami Vijnanananda's room. I saw him seated on a chair. Then he gave me my *diksha-mantra* (the holy name of God). While enunciating the mantra, he slowly swayed back and forth in his chair. This is how I was initiated by him."

One senior swami of our Order, Deven Maharaj, told us about his interesting meeting with Swami Vijnanananda at the Allahabad Ramakrishna ashrama. At that time Deven Maharaj was a young monk. Both Deven Maharaj's and Swami Vijnanananda's mother tongue was Bengali. There are three different "you"s in the Bengali language. The first one is *apni*. It is used for people who are treated with great respect. The second one is *tumi*. It is used for friends and relatives of the same age group, as well as for those who are younger. The third one is *tui*. It is generally addressed to one who is very intimate or younger. It may also be used in regard to those who are of lower social standing.

From the first meeting, for some strange reason, Swami Vijnanananda respectfully addressed Deven Maharaj using apni. This embarrassed him very much. But Swami Vijnanananda appeared to be so grave that Deven Maharaj didn't have the courage to request him to use tumi instead of apni.

Then came the time for the mid-day meal. Swami Vijnana-nanda was a large person, and all the utensils, plates, bowls, and glasses that he used were also quite large. Deven Maharaj was served large portions of lentils, cooked vegetables, milk, etc. in those large bowls. After the food was served, Swami Vijnanananda told Deven Maharaj, "Eat."

But Deven Maharaj was a small man and felt that the quantity of food was too much for him. So he said to Swami Vijnanananda, "Maharaj, this is too much food, I can't eat this much."

Swami Vijnanananda said, "What? You want to disobey your elders!"

So Deven Maharaj was forced to eat all the food.

One may wonder why Swami Vijnanananda behaved that way with Deven Maharaj. Was he whimsical? Swami Brahma-nanda has given the answer to this question. He once said about Swami Vijnanananda, "He is a hidden *brahmajnani*."[6] For some reason best known to himself, Swami Vijnanananda didn't want others to know of his great spirituality. His enigmatic behavior was one of the many disguises he used to hide his spirituality.

THE LESSON IN OBEDIENCE THAT SWAMI BRAHMANANDA TAUGHT SWAMI VIRESWARANANDA

Belur Math is situated on the bank of the holy river Ganga. Inside the monastery grounds there are three *ghats* on the bank of the river. A ghat is a paved staircase built on a riverbank, with the lower steps submerged in water. Anyone wanting to take a bath can reach the deeper waters of the river by using

---

6. A *brahmajnani* is one who has experienced Brahman (God).

the lower steps. Only monks use one of these three Belur Math ghats. It is called the Monks' Ghat. Visitors use the other two. In the dry summer months the water of the river sometimes turns saline because of the tide. But that doesn't diminish the holiness of the river, and a large number of people come to bathe as usual. All this information is necessary to understand the incident that I am now going to narrate to you.

In Belur Math it is a tradition that monks who have newly taken their vows of brahmacharya or sannyasa should go to the senior monks and seek their blessings. The senior monks are then requested to say a few inspirational words. So those of us who had taken the vows of brahmacharya approached Swami Vireswarananda for his blessings after the ceremony was over. Then he told us the following story:

"I was then a newly admitted, young brahmachari (novice) living in Belur Math. One day I went with some other monks to take a bath in the Ganga. We took our bath at the Monks' Ghat on the east side of our original monastery. While going to the river we saw Swamis Brahmananda and Premananda sitting on a bench on the eastern veranda of the monastery.

"After finishing my bath, as I was going past the swamis, Swami Brahmananda told me, 'Go to the river and see if the river water is saline today.'

"While taking my bath, I had already tasted the water. So I said, 'Maharaj, the water today is quite saline.'

"Hearing my reply, Swami Brahmananda became extremely grave. He said, 'I didn't ask you that!'

"I realized that I must have done something wrong. I returned to the river, tasted the water again, and coming back to Swami Brahmananda said, 'Maharaj, the water is saline; I've tasted it.'

"Swami Brahmananda showed total indifference to what I had said. It appeared as though he hadn't even heard my words. His face was awe-inspiringly grave. So I silently left and went back to my room. Later I understood that Swami Brahmananda wanted to teach me a lesson in obedience. He wanted to teach me that a monk, for his own spiritual benefit, should follow the orders of his guru or respected elders without question. Swami Brahmananda had seen me coming out of the river. Still he asked me to go to the river again and taste the water. But I didn't do it. That's why he had behaved with me that way. Truly speaking, he had no interest whatsoever in knowing if the water was saline or not. All that he wanted was to teach me a valuable lesson in obedience."

SOME SPECIALTIES OF THE DISCIPLES OF SRI RAMAKRISHNA

Swami Gangeshananda was the secretary of Swami Shivananda for a number of years. One day he was talking to us about the disciples of Sri Ramakrishna whom he had known. He said, "They very much loved and trusted one another. Mahapurush Maharaj (Swami Shivananda) trusted me completely in money matters, and would also tell others that I could massage very well. Why would he say that? Because, as he himself would explain, 'Raja (Swami Brahmananda) told me that Dwijen (Swami Gangeshananda) can massage very well, and can be completely trusted in money matters.' He had implicit faith in the words of his brother disciple, Swami Brahmananda.

"Once Sri Ramakrishna's disciples would form a good opinion of anyone nothing could dislodge that notion easily. Even if that person committed an offence, they wouldn't notice it. Otherwise, how could they have tolerated a person like me?" (This last statement of Swami Gangeshananda about himself should not be taken seriously. It is only an expression of his humility.)

"Oh, how liberal they were! Mahapurush Maharaj knew my fondness for the game of cricket. When there was going to be a good cricket match in Calcutta, he would give me money and say, 'Go, buy a ticket, and enjoy the game.' After my return, he would ask me for a detailed description of the match. Truly speaking, he had no personal interest in these mundane things. Like the other disciples of Sri Ramakrishna, he had a natural tendency to remain absorbed in spiritual thoughts. But out of love and compassion, he would sometimes come down to my level of childish secular interest and inquire about cricket games."

SAINTS DO NOT CRAVE POWER AND POSITION

When Swami Vishuddhananda, then Vice-President of the global Ramakrishna Order, was asked to give spiritual initiation to devotees by Swami Sankarananda, the then President of the Ramakrishna Order, out of genuine humility he responded, "I can't play the role of a guru. I don't think I'm fit to give spiritual initiation to anybody."

Swami Sankarananda said, "None of us is fit to be a guru, but Sri Ramakrishna likes to play with counterfeit coins. Even though we aren't fit, he gets his work done by using us. That's his glory!"

Both Swami Sankarananda and Swami Vishuddhananda were saints of great spirituality. They were protected from the craving for power and position by their shields of humility. This wonderful tradition of the Ramakrishna Order started with Sri Ramakrishna Himself. On one occasion when a devotee was staying overnight with him in the same room, the devotee was awakened around midnight by some noise in the room. Opening his eyes, he saw that Sri Ramakrishna was wide-awake and passionately and repeatedly entreating the Divine Mother, "Mother, please don't give me name and fame! I am begging you, please don't!"

Sri Ramakrishna also used to say, "Nahang nahang, tuhu tuhu." ("Not I, not I; it's Thou, it's Thou!") This self-abnegation, this wiping out of the false ego, is the hallmark of the Ramakrishna tradition.

When Swami Shivananda, President of the Ramakrishna Order and a saintly disciple of Sri Ramakrishna, passed away, some of his disciples wanted to convert his bedroom in Belur Math (monastery) into a shrine. Their argument was that as the great Swami Vivekananda's bedroom in the monastery had been converted into a shrine, Swami Shivananda's bedroom should also be likewise converted.

This worried the trustees of the Order. Had it been allowed, it would have set a new tradition. Eventually all the rooms of the monastery would have to be converted into shrines, because over the years the Order was going to have many Presidents. So that could not be allowed to happen. Yet, the trustees couldn't make up their minds about what to do. They didn't know how to avoid hurting the feelings of the numerous disciples of Swami Shivananda.

With his demise a vacancy was created in the position of the Order's President, and Swami Akhandananda (1864–1937), another saintly disciple of Sri Ramakrishna, was elected President. The swami used to live in the Sargachhi ashrama, about 80 miles away from Belur Math. Hearing of this problem, he straightaway came to Belur, and carrying his bedroll, entered Swami Shivananda's room. Then he announced, "I'll stay in my big brother's room; let me see who can push me out!" This is how Swami Akhandananda very intelligently solved that difficult and delicate problem.

Aside from being extremely witty the swami was also endowed with great humility. Even though he had been elected President, his humility created a great reluctance in him to play the role of a guru. Only the President or the Vice-Presidents, other than some swamis working outside India, are permitted in the Ramakrishna Order to become a guru. Many devotees were eager to have spiritual initiation from the President of the Ramakrishna Order. But Swami Akhandananda showed no interest whatsoever in initiating anybody.

Several days passed. The trustees of the Order were at a loss to decide how to persuade Swami Akhandananda to give spiritual initiation. Then they remembered that the swami had a special fondness for a junior swami named Shivaswarupananda (1902–1991). He sometimes took care of Swami Akhandananda's meals, and ran errands for him during his occasional visits to Belur Math. The trustees asked Swami Shivaswarupananda to try and persuade Swami Akhandananda to give spiritual initiation.

Accordingly, Swami Shivaswarupananda went to Swami Akhandananda, and after saluting him said, "Many devotees are eager to have spiritual initiation. Will you be gracious enough to bless them with initiation?"

Swami Akhandananda replied, "A disciple of Swami Shivananda gave him a nice silk *dhoti* (a piece of cloth used like a sarong by many men in India), and a silk *chuddar* (wrapper). If I get similar clothes, then I'll consider giving spiritual initiation to the devotees."

Swami Shivaswarupananda gave this information to the trustees. After a while the silk clothes were acquired and given to Swami Akhandananda. But the swami didn't give the slightest hint that he would initiate anybody.

Again the trustees asked Swami Shivaswarupananda to approach Swami Akhandananda. This time Swami Akhandananda said, "Swami Shivananda used to wear a pair of special slippers. The soles were made of rope and the upper part was made of velvet. If I get a similar pair of slippers, I'll consider whether or not to give spiritual initiation."

Those handmade slippers were available only in Nepal. It took several months to procure a pair. This time the swami agreed to give spiritual initiation. But he asked, "To whom will I give spiritual initiation? Where are the devotees? They hardly know me!"

Swami Shivaswarupananda replied, "Many devotees prayed to Swami Shivananda for spiritual initiation, but he was suffering from his last illness and couldn't initiate them. We have a list of those devotees; they'll feel blessed if you initiate them."

The swami then started giving initiation. But he would lay down conditions to be fulfilled by the devotees before he would agree to initiate them. For example, he would ask some married couples to vow to remain like brother and sister after initiation. Sometimes he would ask young, unmarried men to vow to lead a life of complete celibacy after their spiritual initiation.

After hearing the story, I asked Swami Shivaswarupananda, "What happened to those devotees? Did they all agree to take those vows?"

Swami Shivaswarupananda replied, "I don't know about everybody. But I'm sure those who sincerely craved spiritual initiation did."

Life in Indian Monasteries

⌛ GOD ANSWERS UNSELFISH PRAYERS

Swami Pranavatmananda (1904–1975), also known as Pashupati Maharaj, was on a pilgrimage to Kashmir. A brother monk, another swami, accompanied him. One day after traveling many miles on foot, they arrived in the late afternoon at a village high up in the mountains. They were both tired and needed rest. They also needed shelter for the night. Soon they drew the attention of a villager who invited them to stay at his home.

Their host was a Hindu, though most of the people in the village were Muslims. After the two swamis were settled in a room in the villager's house, their host saluted the swamis with folded hands, and with great feeling said to them, "Revered sirs, we haven't had rain for the past few months. Unless the rains come, we shall lose all our crops and will starve. You are *sadhus* (holy men). You have yogic powers. Please bring us rain." So saying, the man left.

By then the sun had set and darkness had descended on the mountain village. For the Hindus it was the hour of evening prayer. Swami Pranavatmananda said to his companion, "Look at that villager's faith in us! He thinks that we can bring rain for them. But we don't have occult powers, and as devotees of Sri Ramakrishna, we don't crave them. It seems we've no other recourse but to pray to Sri Ramakrishna. If He so desires, He can bring rain."

Then the two swamis bolted the door of their room, sat on their prayer rugs, and started praying to Sri Ramakrishna with great devotion. They were so deeply immersed in their prayers that they lost track of time. Suddenly they heard a loud knock at the door. When they opened the door, their host rushed in and fell flat at their feet. Crying out of emotion he said, "The rains have come. It's been raining in torrents for the past one hour, and it's still raining. It's you who have brought this rain for us. I'm going to tell all the villagers about you." Without waiting for a response from the swamis, he then bolted out of the room.

Sometime later he returned soaking wet from the heavy downpour. He brought along with him many villagers—both Hindus and Muslims—to show them the holy men who had brought rain to their village! The swamis said to them, "We haven't brought the rain, it's God who has done it." But the villagers were 100% convinced that it was the two swamis who had brought the rain and saved them.

The next morning the swamis wanted to leave the village, but the villagers wouldn't let them go. With eyes filled with tears they begged the swamis again and again to stay permanently in their village. From then on they wouldn't let the swamis out of their sight. Even though the swamis had very few wants, the villagers tried to pamper them with food and whatever services they could render.

After two or three days, Swami Pranavatmananda said to his companion, "It looks like our only option is to sneak away from this village at midnight, when they are sleeping. In a day or two we'll have a full moon. We have to take advantage of that. We may be able to make our way down the mountain road by moonlight without too much difficulty." As planned, at midnight during the full moon, when the villagers were fast asleep, the two swamis quietly left the village never to return.

I heard this story from Swami Pranavatmananda in India.

🔯 WISDOM VERSUS ETHICAL BEHAVIOR

Once, while I was still a brahmachari, a senior monk named Swami Viswavedananda (1906–1978) told me his experiences as a wandering monk in the Himalayas.

He said, "I was then staying for a few days in a mountain village on the shore of a lake. The villagers were simple-hearted people, completely artless, and uncontaminated by the taint of urban culture. Most had never left their village. They earned their livelihood by farming and raising livestock. They had a small temple in their village that acted as the hub of their community's activities. In the evening, after taking their meals, they would go to the temple and sing religious songs, accompanied by drums and cymbals, for hours together. That was their only recreation.

"One day around dusk, several villagers entered my hut. They looked very excited. The chief of the village was among them. He saluted me and said, 'Maharaj (revered sir), a miracle has happened. Seshnag has appeared in our lake. Please come and see him.'"

The swami continued, "You all know that our religious mythology tells us about the legendary king of snakes, Vasuki, also called Seshnag. The villagers had heard stories from Hindu mythology, and to most of them the mythological characters were real. With some disbelief and a lot of curiosity, I went with them to the lake. There at a distance, I could see a mud hen in the water. Most of its body was hidden under the water, but the head on its slender neck was visible and resembled the hood of a snake. Mud hens are a rare phenomenon in that part of the country. They usually are only seen in lakes and ponds at lower altitudes. With childlike simplicity, the village chief pointed to the mud hen and said to me, 'Maharaj, can you see the hood of Seshnag? Isn't it wonderful that Seshnag has appeared in our village?' I didn't want to correct his mistake. I let him believe that Seshnag had really appeared before them."

Hearing this, I protested, "But it was not right. You should have told them the truth. You should have told them that what they had seen was not Seshnag, but a mud hen."

The elderly swami responded, "I didn't want to create doubts in their minds. They live in a world where the gods, goddesses and mythological characters are all real. Had they started doubting even one thing, they would have ended up becoming agnostics and faithless like the city people. I didn't want to disturb their childlike faith, because that kind of faith alone would eventually bring them closer to God."

I couldn't see eye to eye with the swami then. I couldn't accept what he had said. But now that I have grown in years, I realize that the swami was right and I was wrong. In my younger days, more than anything else, it was my heartless, moral arrogance that stood in the way of appreciating the elderly swami's wisdom—that rare wisdom that comes out of genuine compassion for humanity.

⧗ SOMETIMES IT IS BETTER TO TAKE THE BLAME FOR DOING THE RIGHT THING

The following incident took place in 1958, during the first few months of my joining the monastic Order. I was then in the Shillong ashrama of the Ramakrishna Order in the Khasi and Jaintia Hills in India. A swami managed the ashrama kitchen and took care of the guests. My first assignment as a brahmachari was to act as his assistant. The swami was very fastidious about observing the ashrama protocol. I was expected to consult him about everything I had to do in regard to either the kitchen or the guests. At first, as I was new to the ashrama, I didn't know about this protocol and would arbitrarily make decisions in regard to my work, without prior permission from the swami. This displeased him very much, and he made no secret of it to me. As a result, I decided to consult him for every single little thing I had to do concerning the kitchen and guests.

One afternoon some guests arrived from a town nearly four hundred miles away from Shillong—a trip that had taken nearly twenty-four hours by train and bus. Naturally, they were quite tired and hungry. In such a situation, we would always give the guests some refreshments first, and then take them to the rooms where they would be staying. But I didn't do any of that. The swami in charge of the guests and kitchen was away buying groceries for the ashrama. I decided to wait for his return before doing anything for the guests. A senior monk, Swami Gahanananda, was the manager of the ashrama. When he noticed that I hadn't given any refreshments to the guests, he asked me, "Why haven't you given refreshments to them?"

SWAMI GAHANANANDA

I replied, "I'm waiting for the swami in charge of the kitchen to return from the market. He doesn't approve of my doing things on my own. If I don't take his permission first, he becomes displeased."

Swami Gahanananda said, "The ashrama belongs to God. The devotees who have come are His guests. Shouldn't we take care of them? Go ahead and give them refreshments even if the swami in charge of the kitchen becomes displeased. Sometimes it is better to take the blame for doing the right thing."

⧗ AN IMPORTANT LESSON FOR MONASTICS

Shortly after my joining the Shillong ashrama as a brahmachari, I got an upset stomach and didn't go to the dining room for my meals. Swami Gahanananda, who was the manager of the ashrama, noticed my absence. He came to my room and asked, "What happened? Why didn't you go for your meals?"

I replied, "I have an upset stomach."

"Did you see the doctor of the monastery?" he asked.

I answered in the negative, and said that it was not necessary for me to see a doctor, because I would be all right in a day or two. Then Swami Gahanananda pointed his finger at my body, and asked, "Whose body is that?"

"It's my body," I replied.

He said, "Yes, it used to be your body. However, from the day you joined the Ramakrishna Order it has become Sri Ramakrishna's property. You have no right to either misuse or neglect it."

His words gave me new light. Since that day, I have tried not to abuse or neglect my body. At the same time, I have understood that I must not worship it either. If the need arises, I must be prepared to sacrifice it for a greater cause. I am sure Sri Ramakrishna will gladly approve of that sacrifice.

[Swami Gahanananda is now the senior Vice-President of the Ramakrishna Order.]

⌛ EVERYTHING HAPPENS ACCORDING TO GOD'S WILL

The following incident occurred when I was a brahmachari at the Training Center in Belur Math. We brahmacharis weren't having any of our usual daily classes because it was Sunday. Sunday was also the day we washed our clothes. There were two or three taps (faucets) around the Training Center building. Some of us were busy that day hand-washing our clothes, sitting around one of the taps. Near the tap was the flower garden of the Training Center. The flowers would mainly be used for worship in the large temple of Sri Ramakrishna in Belur Math (Belur Monastery).

An elderly swami named Swami Gopalananda used to come every day to the Training Center with a small basket in his hand to pluck flowers. He had a little shrine in his room. He would decorate his shrine with those flowers. The swami's chosen deity was Gopala or Baby Krishna. In his shrine there was a little metal image of Baby Krishna whom he worshiped with great love and devotion.

While in the Training Center, we brahmacharis used to serve food to the monks in the dining hall of the monastery. Swami Gopalananda would not sit with the other monks in the dining hall to eat his meals. He would bring a small tiffin-carrier into which we used to put his food. He would usually enter the dining hall just as we would start serving food to the monks. But he was so humble that he would wait, and would not allow us to put food into his tiffin-carrier until the main dishes had been served to all other monks. Then he would carry the food to his room, and after offering it to God (Gopala), would eat the sanctified food *(prasad)*.

The swami was childlike by nature. He was very gentle, and would rarely talk. Every morning he would come to the flower garden, silently pluck a few flowers, and then return to his room. That particular day, while washing our clothes, young and talkative as we were, we were loudly discussing the doctrine of karma between ourselves. Swami Gopalananda was passing by. He stopped for a minute and said to us, "The doctrine of karma is nothing. Everything happens according to God's will." Then he quietly walked away.

I had great respect for the swami. I pondered over his words, and then remembered a parable of Sri Ramakrishna about a weaver. The weaver was a very honest and pious soul. Everyone loved and trusted him. He used to sell his goods in the village market, and in that way made a simple living. When a customer asked him the price of a piece of cloth, the weaver would say, "By the will of God the price of the yarn is this much, the labor is so much, and my profit is so much. Therefore, by the will of God, the price of the cloth is so much."

Such was the people's faith in the weaver that the customer would immediately buy the cloth at the quoted price without question.

One day, after taking his evening meal, the weaver was sitting on the porch of his home and chanting the holy name of God. Just then a band of robbers was passing by his house and noticed him. They needed a man to carry the goods they were going to steal. They forced the weaver to accompany them. After committing a robbery in a house, they put a load of stolen goods on the weaver's head to carry. Meanwhile, the police came, but the robbers escaped, leaving behind the weaver. The weaver alone was arrested. He was kept in jail for the night. The next day he was brought before the magistrate for trial. The villagers heard about his arrest and came to the court. They told the magistrate that the weaver could never commit a robbery. The magistrate then asked the weaver to make his statement.

The weaver said, "Your honor, by the will of God I was sitting on the porch of my home and chanting God's holy name. Then, by the will of God, robbers came and forced me to accompany them. By the will of God they robbed a house, and by the will of God they put the stolen goods on my head. Then, by the will of God, the police came and arrested me." The magistrate realized that the weaver was a pious man and ordered his release. On his way home the weaver said to the villagers, "By the will of God I have been released."

Through this parable Sri Ramakrishna was saying that by spiritual practice a state of mind could be achieved when the sense of doer-ship or agency fades away from the mind. The person can no longer think that he or she is the doer. The person gets the unshakeable conviction that God alone is doing everything. He or she is only an instrument in the hands of God. This is a high spiritual state. In this state the doctrine of karma is an invalid doctrine. The doctrine of divine will or the doctrine of predestination is the only valid doctrine.

I believe that Swami Gopalananda, through his devotion must have acquired similar unwavering spiritual conviction about the doctrine of divine will.

⧖ AN EXAMPLE OF PERFECT RELIANCE ON GOD'S WILL

The story I am going to narrate to you is about Swami Vishuddhananda (1883–1962). He was then the Vice-President of our Order. He had come to our Shillong center for a visit. Shillong, being a mile-high city, was cool throughout the year. Swami Vishuddhananda was then in his early seventies. A junior monk named Paritosh was his secretary and personal attendant. Swami Vishuddhananda was a bit sensitive to cold.

While in Shillong he showered every day using warm water. The bathroom that he used belonged to an earlier era and did not have hot water faucets. Water had to be heated in the kitchen and then put in the bathroom every time the swami needed a shower. Paritosh would bring a bucket of steaming hot water from the kitchen and put it in the bathroom. He would also put there a bucket of lukewarm water side by side with a bucket of cold water. When the swami wanted to raise the temperature of the lukewarm water, he could add some of the steaming hot water to it. If he wanted to lower the temperature of the lukewarm water, he could add some cold water to it. The method for taking a shower was to dip a mug in the lukewarm water and then empty it over the body.

Swami Vishuddhananda had recently had cataract surgery. After the surgery he was given special eyeglasses, without which he couldn't see clearly. When he went to take a shower he had to first take off his eyeglasses.

One day he entered the bathroom to take a shower. While inside the dimly lit bathroom, he mistook the steaming hot water for the lukewarm water and poured a mugful on his body. His skin immediately got scalded. He cried out, "Oops! My body is burnt." Then after a moment's pause he said, "No, it's okay. It's the Divine Mother's will."

His attendant was standing outside the door of the bathroom and heard the swami's words. He immediately informed the doctor, and the necessary medical help was given to the swami. That morning the swami was scheduled to give spiritual initiation to some devotees. That had to be postponed for a day.

⧗ DEATH-DEFYING UNSUNG HEROES

The Holy Mother Sri Sarada Devi used to say, "It's worthwhile to learn how to die with dignity." Fear of death is inherent in man. Most people are afraid of death. Yet some extraordinary people display great courage at the time of death. In all my 46 years in the Ramakrishna Order I haven't yet seen a monk who was scared of death. And I have seen many monks die—both old and young.

Our Order had a monk named Brahmachari Jnan Maharaj. He was a disciple of Swami Vivekananda and a lifelong *naishthik* (dedicated) brahmachari. When I saw him he was quite old, most probably in his late eighties. As the last living disciple of Swami Vivekananda, he was highly respected by

BRAHMACHARI JNAN MAHARAJ
(1876–1963)

both the monks and devotees of our Order.

For quite some time he had been suffering from various old-age ailments, but the monks used to say that he would not give up his body without seeing the birth centenary of his guru, Swami Vivekananda. And that's what actually happened. After the birth centenary of Swami Vivekananda in January 1963, Brahmachari Jnan Maharaj's health suddenly turned worse. Then, one day, we heard that his condition had deteriorated so much that he could pass away at any moment. Hearing that news, many brother monks crowded into his room. Seeing them Brahmachari Jnan Maharaj humorously remarked, "Look, somebody is dying and everyone has come to see the fun!"

He passed away shortly thereafter.

Now I would like to tell you about Swami Santoshananda. He was a disciple of the Holy Mother Sarada Devi. When I saw him for the first time, he was most probably in his early seventies. He had a very dignified bearing and his face radiated peace. Most of his life he had been associated with a branch center of our Order called the Ramakrishna Mission Students' Home. This branch center is located in Calcutta. It runs an engineering school and a large students' home for college students, where many financially handicapped students are maintained free of charge. Swami Santoshananda was, at that time, in charge of this educational center.

For health reasons he had to undergo several surgical operations in his old age. Nevertheless, he remained very active and alert. But then his health suddenly took a turn for the worse, and one day he had a heart attack. He called all the other monks of the center and said to them, "I may die today. Let the students be given their dinner early, otherwise my death will interfere with their meal."

His instructions were immediately carried out. The doctor came and was present by his bedside. The swami said to the doctor and others who were present, "It's very interesting. I had heard the expression *death pangs,* but didn't know what it meant. Now I am experiencing them!" He was talking as though he was an impartial observer, watching with interest what was happening to his body! Then he chanted the holy name of God and passed away.

Another interesting story was that of Swami Purushatmananda, otherwise known as Prabuddha Maharaj. He was a disciple of the Holy Mother Sri Sarada Devi and the head of our ashrama in Silchar in India. He was in his late sixties when it was detected that he had lung cancer and an aneurysm of the aorta. He was brought to Calcutta and admitted to Presidency General Hospital. There were several other beds in the room in which he was accommodated.

One evening a few months after his hospitalization, he suddenly sat up in his bed and began to repeat the name of Sri Ramakrishna. A little later he said, "O Holy Mother, you have come! Wait a little, I am coming." Then he said to the nearby

SWAMI PURUSHATMANANDA
(c1895–1962)

patients, "Brothers, are you awake? My time is up. I am going." After this he lay down peacefully on his bed never to rise again.

Then there is the story of Swami Adyananda. At one time he was the head of our Lahore ashrama. When India was partitioned, Lahore went to Pakistan. It became impossible to run the ashrama in Pakistan. So Swami Adyananda moved to India and started a new ashrama in the city of Chandigarh (in Punjab).

The swami was renowned for his keen sense of humor. It was his habit to joke around. Every evening after dinner the monks would have some holy readings. One evening, after the reading, Swami Adyananda cheerfully announced to the monks present, "Tonight I'm going to die." He was apparently in good health, so the monks thought that he was joking as usual. But in the morning they discovered that the swami had died naturally in his sleep.

Another case. Brahmachari Prahlad Maharaj spent most of his monastic life at Belur Math near Calcutta. He was a disciple of Swami Shivananda of the Ramakrishna Order. He had been a gifted singer from the time he was young, and his guru, Swami Shivananda, recognizing his talent, sent him to a newly started music college in the state of Uttar Pradesh in India to get further training in music. When he finished the last year of his training, and was about to take the final examination to get his degree, Swami Shivananda called him back to Belur Math. He said, "You don't need degrees. You are now well trained in music. Come and serve the Lord with your talent."

After he returned to Belur Math, he was asked to lead the daily evening vesper service (called *aratrikam* in India). Every evening many monks and devotees attended the aratrikam held in the shrine. Brahmachari Prahlad Maharaj also sang solos when the occasion called for it. Other than that, he tutored the junior monks who were interested in vocal music.

His whole life he dutifully obeyed whatever his guru had asked him to do. When he was old and in failing health, he retired, and would sing only on rare occasions. Over the years he had developed some heart complications. A time came when he became bedridden. One morning we were informed by the doctor (who was a swami), that the condition of his heart had deteriorated very much, and he might pass away any time that day.

Hearing that, we all went to see Prahlad Maharaj in his room at the monastery. Some of our monks who were good singers were already in his room singing devotional songs, because Prahlad Maharaj loved to hear devotional music. Even though bedridden, he was mentally alert and cheerful. The doctor examined him again and said to the swami in charge of the kitchen, "Let the noon worship in the temple be finished earlier, so that the midday meal can be served to the monks soon. Any further delay will cause a problem, because Prahlad Maharaj is going to pass away in two or three hours."

Hearing that, Prahlad Maharaj said to the doctor, "There's

no need to rush. I'm not going to die that soon. I'll last till the late afternoon." And Prahlad Maharaj was right. He passed away peacefully in the late afternoon.

Srikantha Maharaj was a pharmacist at our charitable clinic in Belur Math. He was a devotee of Sri Krishna. During the festival of Rash Purnima, a discourse on the scripture the *Srimad Bhagavatam* would be given in our temple at Belur Math. One of the scholarly swamis, well versed in the scriptures, would usually conduct the discourse. The *Srimad Bhagavatam,* among other things, describes the divine life of Sri Krishna. Many monks and devotees would come to listen to the discourse. Srikantha Maharaj usually sat in the front row listening intently with his eyes closed. I often saw tears running down his cheeks out of spiritual emotion.

Srikantha Maharaj was not a very sophisticated monk. He was plainspoken and in the habit of speaking unpleasant truths. In spite of his old age, his health was fairly good. One night, very late, he came out of his room and sat on the floor of the open veranda in front of his room. He leaned against the wall of the veranda and began chanting the name of God. Another swami named Swami Ajapananda noticed this and came to Srikantha Maharaj. He asked Srikantha Maharaj, "Is there anything wrong with you? Why are you sitting on the floor like this?"

Srikantha Maharaj didn't answer; he just kept on chanting the holy words *Hari Bol* again and again. Then he suddenly collapsed and breathed his last.

Part II

⧗ SWAMI ASIMANANDA AND THE NUN

This incident happened at Belur Math, the headquarters of the Ramakrishna Order in India. One afternoon Swami Asimananda (1883–1976), a very senior monk of the Order, was sitting on a bench in front of the headquarters office, as he usually did every day. The swami was very much venerated and loved for his serene, childlike, yet intelligent nature.

A wandering *bhairavi* (Tantric nun), about 40 years old and with long flowing hair, approached the elderly monk. She was holding a trident in her hand. After greeting the swami, she said, "Swamiji, may I ask you a question?"

Without speaking the swami nodded his assent and she proceeded to ask him an elaborate spiritual question. Swami Asimananda with his natural simplicity, asked, "Mother, why don't you answer your own question?"

BHASKAR PURI

The bhairavi then turned, looked at her trident, and addressing it by the name of "Omkar" said, "Omkar, should I answer, or should you answer?"

Apparently listening to a reply that only she could hear, she said, "I see, you want *me* to answer the question. Okay." She then proceeded to answer her own question with a long and involved explanation. She then

49

said, "Swamiji, may I ask you another question?"

Swami Asimananda silently nodded his assent, and she once again asked a highly intricate spiritual question. The swami then repeated, "Mother, why don't you please answer your own question?"

She turned to her trident, Omkar, and said, "Omkar, should I answer the question or should you?"

After a pause, she said, "Oh, you want me to answer again!" Then she gave another complex reply to her own question. After answering her own question, she happily saluted Swami Asimananda and said, "Swamiji, thank you! You have really helped me a lot." Then she left, content and satisfied with the interview. Swami Asimananda went on quietly sitting there.

Swami Saswatananda, then the Assistant General Secretary of the Ramakrishna Order, observed this incident from a distance. He told us this story.

⧗ REMINISCENCES ABOUT SWAMI GAMBHIRANANDA

I spent ten wonderful years with Swami Gambhirananda at our headquarters office in Belur Math, India. I saw him day in and day out. For several years I lived in the same office building where he lived. If you associate with someone closely, as time passes by, you sometimes lose your initial respect for that person. But the more closely I came to know Swami Gambhirananda over the years, the more my respect grew for him.

The greatness of those who lead a monastic life is revealed more through the little things they do, than what they do in a big way. I knew well that Swami Gambhirananda was a very capable administrator, a great scholar, a great author, an ac-

SWAMI GAMBHIRANANDA
(1898–1989)

complished speaker, etc. He was also a very austere monk with very few possessions. But what impressed me most were some minor, but highly revealing incidents in his life. I am going to narrate some of them to you.

When I was with him at the headquarters office he was the General Secretary, the chief executive of the Order. Some fifteen monks worked under him in his office. Later he became the 11th President, the spiritual head, of the Ramakrishna Order.

He had an extremely sharp mind that enabled him to work very fast. Nearly fifty letters would come for him every day. He would sort the letters, and mark them for monks working in the different departments of his office. He would draft replies by hand to numerous letters every day within an hour or two, and deliver the drafts to me to make sure that the monk who did the typing typed them correctly. The typed letters would be sent to him later for his signature and then mailed.

After distributing the letters to the different departments (he would not take the help of the office boys for this), he would then sit on a bench in front of our office building for a while, wearing his usual, simple clothes. Had a newcomer seen him at that time, it would be hard for that person to even imagine that he was the chief executive of the global Ramakrishna Order. After sitting on the bench for half an hour or so, he would go back to his desk in the office upstairs.

He taught us not to waste anything, because the money donated by the devotees was not to be misused. That's how we got used to extreme austerity in the use of office stationery. Swami Gambhirananda would open his mail and then would use the blank inner sides of the used envelopes as drafting paper! Eventually a printing press started giving us their rejected paper, which we would use to draft letters.

In between his office work, he would write books. He had written, among others, a two-volume Bengali book entitled *Yuganayak Vivekananda*. The Udbodhan office in Calcutta, a publishing center of the Ramakrishna Order, published the book. Swami Vishwashrayananda (1916–1978) was the head of that center. He came one day to the headquarters office with copies of the newly published *Yuganayak Vivekananda*. He entered Swami Gambhirananda's office, placed the volumes on the swami's desk, and saluted him. Swami Gambhirananda greeted him with a pleasant smile. Then Swami Vishwashrayananda said with great feeling, "Maharaj (revered sir), you have been doing a great service to our Order by writing these books!"

Until Swami Vishwashrayananda had said those words, Swami Gambhirananda had had a smile on his face. But as soon as he heard that, his face became stern, and he roared, "You are saying that I've been doing a great service to the Order! How do you know that I've not been writing these books to bolster my false ego?"

Swami Vishwashrayananda replied with folded hands, "Maharaj, please forgive me; I made a mistake." Swami Gambhirananda's face immediately became pleasant again.

I was present in Swami Gambhirananda's office and witnessed the whole incident. The behavior of Swami Gambhirananda convinced me that he was completely free from that false ego that inspires many authors to write. Swami Vishwashrayananda was also similarly convinced.

In this connection I would like to narrate a sad incident about another swami. Swami Vivekananda once said that the craving for name and fame was the last infirmity of noble souls. A person may make immense spiritual progress, and yet get stuck in the craving for name and fame. Ordinary people crave sense pleasure and wealth more than name and fame. Spiritually evolved people may become free from that craving, but may still crave name and fame.

The swami I am talking about was a very pure soul. He was highly educated with more than one postgraduate degree from a renowned university. He had written several scholarly books on religious topics, and all of them were published by our Order. He was honest, kind and truthful, and his lifestyle was austere. We all respected him.

When he was in his early seventies, an American publisher showed interest in publishing one of his books in America. As our Order had the copyright, the swami went to our General Secretary seeking permission to have the book published by the American publisher. When approached, the General Secretary said that it was not within his power to give permission. He said that only when the copyright period had expired could other publishers publish his book, otherwise not. But the swami was adamant. He pestered the General Secretary again and again for permission to publish the book in America.

Finally the General Secretary said to him, "Your book is the property of our Order. If you want to have your books published by outside publishers, the only way you can do it is by writing books while outside the Order." The swami felt hurt at the General Secretary's words and quietly left the Order.

First he went to his nephew's home in Calcutta. But having spent the major part of his life in a monastery, he felt most uncomfortable in a family atmosphere. So he went to Varanasi and found accommodation in a place where wandering monks are allowed to stay. The swami stayed in a little unfurnished room and fed himself by begging food from people's homes. (In India it is customary for wandering monks to beg food from people's homes.)

We have two branch centers in Varanasi. One of them is a hospital center. It runs a large charitable hospital. The monks of those two centers tried to persuade the swami to come back to our Order, but he refused. Nevertheless, they kept watch over him. After a few months' stay in Varanasi, the swami became seriously ill. He was completely bedridden and unable to walk. The monks of our hospital center brought him by stretcher to our hospital. The swami said to the monks, "Why have you brought me here? I've left the Order."

The monks said, "You may have left the Order, but the Order hasn't left you!"

The swami was given all kinds of medical help but he didn't recover. After staying in the hospital for a month or two, he passed away peacefully. Our monks took care of his funeral.

This sad story illustrates how a spiritually evolved soul may get stuck in the trap of fame and public recognition. Swami Gambhirananda was free from that allurement.

He had a beautiful way of teaching the junior monks. Once he noticed that I would leave my room unlocked. Since we lived in the upstairs of our office building next to a public thoroughfare, it was all the more necessary that the rooms should be kept locked. The only possessions that I had in my room were a few religious books, three sets of monastic clothes, and a small, rickety table fan. The age of the fan was far greater than mine! Surprisingly, it still worked!

Swami Gambhirananda asked me, "Why don't you lock your room regularly?"

I replied, "I don't have anything valuable in my room. That's why I don't lock my room."

He said, "It's better to lock it up; otherwise, you become responsible for luring poor people to come and steal."

Thus advised, I started locking the door of my room. But one day, by mistake, I left my room unlocked and went elsewhere. When I returned, I found the door of my room locked. I asked one of the office boys, "Who has locked my room?"

He replied, "Swami Gambhirananda has done it."

I felt extremely embarrassed. I asked the office boy, "Where is the key?"

He replied, "It's with Swami Gambhirananda."

I entered Swami Gambhirananda's room. He was sitting in an old reclining camp chair with his eyes closed. He often would be found that way when he wanted to sit quietly and think. As soon as he heard my footsteps, he said with his eyes still closed, "The key is on the desk." He didn't scold me or anything, but he taught me a lesson that I never forgot. In the ashrama in Seattle, where I have lived for the past thirty years, I always lock the door of my room when I go out. Some people think that it's funny. But I do it out of reverence for Swami Gambhirananda, who taught me a valuable lesson nearly thirty-four years ago.

Swami Gambhirananda had extraordinary concentration of mind. I would like to tell you a story about this. In Belur Math, tea is served to the monks twice a day—once in the morning during breakfast, and again around 3 o' clock in the afternoon. Those of us who worked in the headquarters office used to be served the afternoon tea in our office by a servant. The tea, however, would be prepared in the main kitchen of the monastery. The servant would go to the kitchen and bring back a large kettleful of tea for us. He would first serve tea to Swami Gambhirananda and then to the rest of us.

One afternoon, the cook who prepared tea in the kitchen mistook the salt for sugar and put it in the tea. As soon as we took the first sip, we could taste the salt and immediately poured that terribly salty tea out of our cups. Meanwhile the young swami in charge of the kitchen came running to our office, apologized profusely for the mistake, and said that fresh tea was being prepared and would be served shortly.

I then went upstairs to Swami Gambhirananda's room to give him that information. I found him sitting in his old, reclining camp chair with his eyes closed. As mentioned earlier, when he used to think deeply about something, he would sometimes shut his eyes like that. When I entered his room, he opened his eyes and looked at me inquiringly. I said, "Maharaj (revered sir), the salty tea that you got is going to be replaced with fresh tea. Please give me your cup, I'll empty it down the sink and rinse the cup."

In amazement, he asked, "What salty tea? I drank the whole cup of tea that was given to me. I didn't know it had salt in it!"

Now it was my turn to be amazed. I understood that as he was drinking his tea, he must have been thinking of something with such great concentration that he hadn't tasted the salt in the tea.

Swami Gambhirananda was very straightforward. Some wrongly interpreted this straightforwardness as a lack of feeling for others. Those of us who had the opportunity to be close to him knew him to be a person with great feeling for others. But he would not verbally express his feelings. He *acted* on his feelings. When I first came to work at the headquarters office he said, "You see, you have now come to work in a place that deals with the monks of our Order. You have to learn to treat them with brotherly love. You should remember this when you send official letters to them. Paid employees work in government offices. They can afford to be heartless. But we are different. In our Order, we deal with our brother monks who are all volunteers."

Once a junior monk of one of our South Indian centers had gone to a different city to collect donations for his center. Unfortunately, he contracted infectious hepatitis from drinking contaminated water and had to be hospitalized. The hospital bill ran pretty high. The swami in charge of the center to which the monk belonged said that as the center's finances were pretty bad, the monk should try to collect donations to pay his bill. Though released from the hospital, the monk was still weak and couldn't think of traveling again to collect donations. He wrote a letter to Swami Gambhirananda describing his predicament.

Swami Gambhirananda was very moved after reading his letter. He said to me, "See how heartless people are! This poor boy is being forced to collect money to pay his hospital bill!" Then he asked the cashier of the headquarters to send money to pay the bill.

Belur Math had many retired monks living there. Some of them were suffering from different old-age conditions. But due to paucity of funds, they couldn't be given proper medical care. Many had to silently suffer from illnesses that could have been cured, given the proper treatment. Due to paucity of funds, this problem was neglected for many years.

It was Swami Gambhirananda who first decided to do something about it. He created a fund to treat the sick and elderly monks of the Order. At his inspiration, many donors came forward and donated substantial sums to the fund. He also created a convalescence home for monks called *Arogya Bhavan* that could accommodate a fair number of ailing monks. Had he not had special feeling for suffering monks, he wouldn't have tried to make such arrangements.

While performing his duties as the General Secretary of the Ramakrishna Order, he gave maximum importance to whatever was in the best interests of the Order. He believed in the pyramid style of administration. He understood that for smooth running of the organization, he should depend on his subordinates, such as the heads of branch centers. He had not arbitrarily chosen these heads. The governing body of the Order appointed them. Only capable monks were put in charge of the centers.

Swami Gambhirananda expected that a monk of a branch center should first approach the head of the center with all his work-related problems. For example, if a monk wanted a transfer elsewhere, he was expected to first talk about this with the head of the center to which he was attached. He was not supposed to write directly to the General Secretary requesting a transfer. All the monks knew this policy of the headquarters. Nevertheless, if a monk did write directly to the General Secretary requesting a transfer without first talking to the head, he would be instructed by the General Secretary to approach the headquarters through the head of his center.

Without following this procedure, one monk who was the cashier and accountant of a fairly large educational center, wrote directly to the General Secretary for a transfer. Swami Gambhirananda asked the monk to send his request through the proper channel, i.e. through the head of his center. But the monk didn't do it. One morning he arrived unannounced at the headquarters office. Swami Gambhirananda was then on the ground floor of the office. He had come down from his private office upstairs. The monk saluted Swami Gambhirananda. With a smile on his face Swami Gambhirananda greeted him and said, "You didn't inform us that you would be coming today. Is everything all right with your center?"

The monk said, "I've left that center. I'm not going back. I want a transfer."

Hearing this Swami Gambhirananda became very displeased. He told the monk sternly, "You left your work unattended there. You will never get a transfer that way! You must return to your center at once."

The monk said, "Please excuse me, Maharaj, I can't do that!"

Swami Gambhirananda raised his voice and said sternly, "If you won't go back you have to leave the Order!"

Some of us who were in the office at the time and had been listening to the conversation felt extremely sorry for the monk, and wondered why Swami Gambhirananda had treated the monk so heartlessly.

The monk saluted Swami Gambhirananda and quietly left the headquarters office. The monk was senior to me in monastic life by several years. I followed him outside and after saluting him said, "Maharaj, What will you do now? Where will you go?"

He replied, "I am going to Calcutta (nearly 4 miles away), there I'll meet a brother monk and then decide where I'll go." I accompanied him to the bus stand and sadly watched him board a bus and disappear from sight.

When I returned to the headquarters office, Swami Gambhirananda was still on the ground floor of the office. He asked us, "Where is he? Is he gone?" We didn't reply. We all kept quiet. Then he said, "Doesn't he have any friends here?" Still there was silence. Swami Gambhirananda then went upstairs to his private office.

Swami Gambhirananda's stern behavior toward the swami was obviously meant to give him some kind of shock therapy. Swami Gambhirananda knew more than anyone else that it was not within his power to ask any monk to leave the Order for a minor breach of discipline. Such decisions could only be made by the governing body of the Order.

The brother monk in Calcutta persuaded the monk to return to his center. We at the headquarters were very relieved to hear the news. After returning to his center, he didn't try for a transfer again.

Part II

Nearly a month after this incident, Swami Gambhirananda went on an official tour of several centers. He asked me to accompany him. The center from which the above-mentioned monk had come was one of those we visited. After our arrival there by car, Swami Gambhirananda greeted the monk with a warm smile and behaved as though the incident at the headquarters office had never happened. He even invited him to accompany us on our visit to another center a few hundred miles away.

Sometimes to maintain organizational discipline, Swami Gambhirananda had to behave sternly. But there were never any hard feelings in his heart. Another exemplar in this area was Swami Chidatmananda. He was the junior Assistant General Secretary when Swami Gambhirananda was the General Secretary.

Occasionally, for the sake of monastic discipline, it would become necessary to scold the junior monks. Often Swami Chidatmananda would be asked to carry out this unpleasant duty. He was extremely good-hearted. He had nothing but love and goodwill for the monks. So having to scold them would be all the more painful for him. Nevertheless, out of a sense of duty he would do it. For him, it was painful playacting. I can easily guess that Swami Gambhirananda's feelings were not any different from those of Swami Chidatmananda.

Swami Gambhirananda was a superb administrator. Those of us who worked in his office developed more and more respect for him every day. Even though we were so many years junior to him, he used to refer to us as "colleagues." He would first check us out by giving us responsibilities. When he was satisfied with our performance, he would completely rely on us. His total trust in us encouraged us to give our best for the Order.

As mentioned earlier, Swami Gambhirananda was extremely straightforward. The following incident is one example of Swami Gambhirananda's straightforwardness.

Any new project for a branch center had to be first approved by the headquarters. The proposal had to be submitted to the headquarters for final approval by the members of the governing body. The proposals were approved by democratic vote.

Mr. Avinashilingam was the head of the largest educational center in the Ramakrishna Order. Both he and Swami Gambhirananda were disciples of Swami Shivananda. Mr. Avinashilingam brought a proposal to the headquarters to start an agricultural university at his center. A few minutes before the meeting of the governing body, I heard Mr. Avinashilingam say to Swami Gambhirananda, "The university is a great necessity. You must support my proposal."

Swami Gambhirananda replied, "Brother Avinashi, we don't yet have enough monastic manpower to run a university, so I shall oppose the proposal. But you may talk to the other members of the governing body. If they approve, you will get your university."

The proposal, however, fell through. The governing body did not approve it. To avoid giving an unpleasant answer to Mr. Avinashilingam, Swami Gambhirananda could have given an evasive reply, but his natural straightforwardness did not allow him to do so. Besides that, being a brother disciple, he felt close to Mr. Avinashilingam and could frankly and unhesitatingly tell Mr. Avinashilingam what he had in his mind. Had he been a stranger, Swami Gambhirananda would have talked differently. In dealing with outsiders he always behaved like a perfect gentleman.

This kind of straightforwardness is an asset in spiritual life. Sri Ramakrishna used to say, "Be straightforward; let your words reflect your thoughts." Swami Gambhirananda lived that teaching.

I very rarely heard Swami Gambhirananda talk about his own spiritual experiences. Like most other swamis of our Order, he was reticent about them. Yet, I heard that after his pilgrimage to Amarnath when he was asked, "Were you able to see the ice *lingam* (symbol) of Lord Shiva inside the cave?" he replied, "I'm not sure, I thought I saw Sri Ramakrishna there."

Now I'll narrate another interesting incident. Once a young man wearing western clothes came to Belur Math. His name was Jatin, and he had just arrived in Calcutta by ship from Rangoon. In Rangoon he had worked in the Military Accounts Department of Burma. He had come all the way from Burma to become a monk of the Ramakrishna Order. He wanted to see Swami Shivananda, who was then the President, to get his permission to join the Order. During the meeting Swami Shivananda glanced at the young man's impeccable suit and then told him that he wouldn't be allowed to join. He might have thought that the young man was foppish and therefore not suitable for monastic life.

Jatin left Swami Shivananda's room and sat sadly on a bench on the porch downstairs. He was wondering what he would do next when a middle-aged monk named Swami Nirvedananda arrived. When he saw the sad-looking young man sitting there, he became curious. On inquiry, he came to know the entire story. He then went to Swami Shivananda and said, "Maharaj, I saw a young man sitting downstairs. I've talked to him. He seems to be a very fine young man."

Swami Shivananda then said to Swami Nirvedananda, "Do you think so? Then tell him that he can join the Order."

That young man became a monk, and after holding many responsible positions in the Ramakrishna Order, became its eleventh President. Swami Gambhirananda was that young man. I heard the above story from Swami Bodhatmananda.

⧗ IN MARRIED LIFE *Ours* IS BETTER THAN *His* OR *Hers*

I heard another interesting incident about Swami Gambhirananda. Once he lost much of his vision due to retinal detachment. To regain his sight, he had to go from India to Boston and have eye surgery. At that time surgeons in India could not perform that kind of surgery. Our Boston Vedanta center arranged for the swami's visit to the United States, and a renowned ophthalmologist in Boston performed the surgery.

Mrs. Eleanor Stark, a close devotee of the Boston Vedanta center, writes:

As I was helping at the (Vedanta) center and had a car at that time, I drove Swami Gambhirananda to Massachusetts General Hospital for appointments. Although the swami was (then) virtually blind, he was able somehow to ascertain my speed and cautioned me to go slower!…One day I told the swami about "my husband's garden." "Don't you mean *our* garden?" the swami observed. It was a lesson I never forgot.

The next time I saw the swami was at a large ceremony at Hyderabad (in India) some years later. Swami Gambhirananda heard our voices as he was getting out of the bus of visiting swamis, walked over to us and said, "How is *our* garden?"

⌛ THE ABSENCE OF FALSE EGO IN THE LIVES OF THE SPIRITUALLY EXALTED

One special characteristic that I have noticed in the lives of the exalted monks of our Order is their lack of a false ego. When I was a brahmachari, Swami Vireswarananda had me brought to the headquarters office from our Shillong ashrama. He was then the General Secretary, the chief executive at the headquarters office. Soon after my arrival Swami Vireswarananda said to me, "I've heard that you have had experience in auditing accounts in your pre-monastic life. We need someone to examine the statements of account sent to us by our branch centers. You'll have to do that work."

But I needed a desk and chair. There was a large secretariat table in the correspondence section of our office. One swami used the table as his desk. Swami Vireswarananda said, "You will also use that table for your work. You use one side of the table while the swami will use the other. You'll sit facing each other." But I needed some drawers to put the statements of accounts in. The table was equipped with several drawers on each side. The drawers on my side of the table, however, were not usable, because they were locked. When I brought that fact to the attention of Swami Vireswarananda, he said, "They were used by Swami Asimananda. He is now leading a retired life in our Advaita Ashrama in Varanasi. He must have locked those drawers." Then Swami Vireswarananda found a bunch of keys and started trying them on the locks of the drawers. After several attempts, he found the right key.

When the drawers were pulled out, we discovered that they were all stuffed with letters of various kinds—some of them were official letters, while others were personal letters addressed to Swami Asimananda. Swami Vireswarananda said, "The drawers

SWAMI VIRESWARANANDA
(1892–1985)

have to be emptied for your use." When I wanted to do that, he said, "No, you won't be able to do that. I've got to sort these letters and put them in their proper places." So saying he sat down on the bare cement floor and started sorting the letters.

He didn't mind in the least sitting on that bare floor for about an hour to help a brahmachari who was more than 40 years younger than he. Even though he was the chief executive of the Ramakrishna Order, he was completely oblivious of his exalted official position. That day I learned from him a wonderful practical lesson in humility. I also learned how to completely wipe out one's false ego by a true spirit of dedication and service to God.

I would like to mention here that Swami Vireswarananda later became the tenth President of the Ramakrishna Order.

Another anecdote. Swami Chidatmananda, then the Assistant General Secretary of our Order, used to live with us in the same building in Belur Math. The other residents were very junior monks who used to work in the headquarters office.

Every Sunday our office would be closed, and we usually washed our clothes by hand in the morning. In order not to wet the clothes we were wearing, we would remove our shirts and wrap a towel around our waists. The upper part of the body would remain bare.

One Sunday the junior-most monk in our building was busy washing his clothes. He was extremely skinny. To tease him I said, "You need more flesh on your body. You should eat more."

He replied, "I may be skinny, but I am strong. And besides, I know boxing."

I told him, "Is that true? I don't think you can defend yourself, even if I fight you using only one arm." He accepted my challenge, and tried to hit me using both his fists, but didn't succeed. It was obvious that he had only rudimentary training in boxing.

Swami Chidatmananda was in his room at that time and heard our conversation. He came out, watched our friendly fight for a minute or so, and then said to me, "You seem to know boxing. I also used to box when I was a young man. Come and fight with me! But on one condition—you won't attack me; you'll only defend yourself." That's how I had a boxing bout with Swami Chidatmananda. However, the fight lasted for only two or three minutes. Swami

SWAMI CHIDATMANANDA
(1910–1975)

67

Chidatmananda was then in his early sixties and I was in my thirties.

Swami Chidatmananda's behaviour that day overwhelms me with inexpressible joy even now. Though highly respected by us for the high position he held in our Order, he sometimes came down to our level and behaved as though he was our pal. In India, where not only official position, but also seniority in age generates great respect, such behavior is unprecedented—except perhaps among the monks in the Ramakrishna Order. Had Swami Chidatmananda been conscious of his high position and seniority in age, he couldn't have behaved that way with us. It was his complete lack of false ego that made such behavior possible.

⧗ MONKS BELONG TO THE ENTIRE WORLD

Once, shortly after I had joined the monastic Order as a young brahmachari, I went to see Swami Premeshananda, an elderly monk of our Order. The swami was a disciple of the Holy Mother Sri Sarada Devi and in his late seventies at that time.

After I saluted him, he asked me, "Where were you born?"

I replied, "In the northeastern part of the country, in the city of Shillong."

"Really?" said the swami, as though surprised at my reply, "How large were you when you were born?"

I replied, "I must have been no larger than an average newly-born baby."

"Good," said the swami. Then he continued, "When you were born you occupied only as little space as an average baby's body would occupy. It's in that little space you were actually born. Why then do you say that you were born in the city of Shillong? Obviously, you were not satisfied with the little, insignificant space in which you were born. That's why you wanted to transcend your limitations. You expanded to include the whole city. But you didn't stop there. You further expanded to include the entire country. You started calling yourself an Indian. But why should you stop there? Why don't you transcend your limits further and include the entire world?

SWAMI PREMESHANANDA
(1884–1967)

"Do you know where we, the monks of the Ramakrishna Order, belong? Ideally speaking, we don't belong to any city, any country, any single race or nation. We belong to a family called humankind. We belong to the entire world. Our God is the God of all nations. Our pains and sorrows are the pains and sorrows of the entire human race. We can never live apart from others, just as they cannot live apart from us. We are always one with them. Our identity with them is based on the omnipresence of God."

⧖ WHAT IS A TRUE MIRACLE?

We have a center in Calcutta named the Advaita Ashrama. A medical doctor lived close to that center. The doctor claimed that he was an atheist. Yet, he loved to come and talk to Swami Chidatmananda, who was then the head of that center. One day he came to see the swami. After taking his seat in the swami's office he said, "Swamiji, I assure you if you show me just one miracle, I'll become a believer."

Just then a young monk entered the swami's office carrying papers for the swami to sign. After the monk left Swami Chidatmananda said to the doctor, "You were asking for a miracle. You've just seen one. Do you believe in God now?"

"What miracle?" asked the doctor in surprise.

"Didn't you see that monk? He is the miracle! He is young, healthy, highly educated, and handsome. He has all the necessary qualifications to succeed in the world. Yet he has chosen to be a monk, leaving behind all the worldly pleasures. Isn't that a miracle?" asked Swami Chidatmananda.

The doctor wasn't convinced, and he remained an atheist. He couldn't see eye to eye with Swami Chidatmananda. He had expected to see some other kind of miracle.

⧖ MIRACLES DO NOT NECESSARILY CONVINCE PEOPLE

A junior monk named Sitangshu was very fond of Brahmachari Jnan Maharaj. As mentioned earlier, Brahmachari Jnan Maharaj was the last living disciple of Swami Vivekananda. When Sitangshu met him, he was already elderly. The monks of the Ramakrishna Order respected Brahmachari Jnan Maharaj for his saintliness and exemplary life.

One characteristic of Brahmachari Jnan Maharaj was that he was equally friendly to both the junior and senior monks of the Order. They would come and talk to him freely, without any reservation. One day Sitangshu came to Brahmachari Jnan Maharaj and said to him, "Maharaj, our scriptures talk about miracles. Can you please show me one? If I see a miracle, my faith in the scriptures will be strengthened."

Brahmachari Jnan Maharaj wouldn't agree. Nevertheless, Sitangshu was insistent. He wouldn't give up. Finally Brahmachari Jnan Maharaj said, "I've no power whatsoever to perform miracles. Nor do I ever want such powers."

Sitangshu replied, "It's so hot today! This is the dry season, and it hasn't rained for so many days! And this morning I've got to go to Calcutta to do some official work for the Order. If it rains today, I'll consider that a miracle."

Brahmachari Jnan Maharaj replied, "If Sri Ramakrishna so wills, rain may come."

By the time Sitangshu finished his work in Calcutta it was late afternoon. As he was about to take the bus to return to Belur Math, it started raining in torrents. It rained so heavily that a few inches of water quickly accumulated on the streets of Calcutta. When Sitangshu reached Belur Math, it was around dusk. After his arrival he remembered that he had requested Brahmachari Jnan Maharaj to bring rain. The rain came, but it failed to generate any faith in Sitangshu's mind. He thought, "It seems the rain would have come anyway."

⧗ FOUR STORIES ABOUT TRUTHFULNESS

I had great respect for Swami Krishnatmananda. He was an exemplary monk. While in the Shillong ashrama I associated with him closely for three years. Once several monks of the Shillong ashrama went to conduct flood relief work in Rangia in the Kamrup district of Assam. I was one of them. When the relief work was over and we were getting ready to return to Shillong, Swami Krishnatmananda came to the relief camp for a day. The distance between Shillong and Rangia is about 120 miles. To reach Shillong, the six members of our relief team would have to go half the way by train and the other half by bus. And that certainly was not going to be a comfortable journey. So Swami Krishnatmananda remarked, "Wouldn't it be nice if someone brings a car and takes us back to Shillong?"

Sri Ramakrishna has said that if a person practices truthfulness for twelve years, whatever comes out of his or her mouth will come true. I heard what Swami Krishnatmananda said and told another monk, "Swami Krishnatmananda has expressed a wish for a car to come and take us back to Shillong. His words must come true. I'm sure a car will come and pick us up."

The monk replied, "Are you crazy? Not a chance! Who will come to pick us up?"

But the monk was wrong. Mr. Shyamapada Chaudhury, Chief Engineer of the Assam State Electricity Board, was passing by the town of Rangia. He came to see us at the relief camp that day and volunteered to take all of us in his large jeep back to Shillong. This is how Swami Krishnatmananda's wish came true.

SWAMI KRISHNATMANANDA
(1906–1996)

Another incident concerns a brahmachari in the Shillong ashrama. He got a used German camera as a gift from someone. With great enthusiasm he procured a roll of film, and wanted to take group pictures of the monks at the ashrama. Swami Krishnatmananda was at that time the ashrama manager. He and several other monks stood together forming a group for the picture taking. Swami Krishnatmananda suddenly remarked, "I doubt if the camera will take even a single picture!" Nevertheless, the brahmachari took several pictures of the group, and the film was given to a photography shop for development. But wonder of wonders! Not a single picture came out. All of them were completely black.

Later it was discovered that an inner layer of dark paper inside the camera had come loose and had obstructed the lens. Even a casual remark of Swami Krishnatmananda would come true. Having known many other similar cases in our Order, I am not the least surprised at this phenomenon.

In this connection, I would like to narrate a third incident. Swami Adinathananda, a disciple of the Holy Mother Sri Sarada Devi, was the head of our Jamshedpur ashrama. One day a lady came to see the swami. She was extremely upset and said to him, "Maharaj, I have lost my cat. Please bless me in order that my cat comes back."

On inquiry the swami came to know that she had lost her cat nearly a month earlier. A cat missing for that many days usually never comes back. But the lady was too upset to realize it. She sat in front of the swami and started crying. To comfort her, Swami Adinathananda said, "Don't worry, your cat will come back."

And wonder of wonders, a few days later the cat really came back. It was just another proof that a truthful person's words come true. But now Swami Adinathananda was in trouble. People in Jamshedpur started thinking that the swami had supernatural powers—the kind of fame that as a monk of the Ramakrishna Order, Swami Adinathananda certainly didn't want.

SWAMI ASESHANANDA
(1899–1996)

The fourth story is about Swami Aseshananda, who was a disciple of the Holy Mother Sri Sarada Devi. For many years the swami was the head of our Vedanta center in Portland, Oregon, in the U.S.A. An interesting incident took place there.

Mr. and Mrs. Freinderich lived in Portland. They had a nine-year-old son who could not walk. One of their acquaintances who knew

Swami Aseshananda and most probably was a devotee of the Portland Ashrama, suggested that they take their ailing son to Swami Aseshananda. As suggested, Mrs. Freinderich took her son to the swami and requested him to pray for her son. Swami Aseshananda looked into the boy's eyes, picked him up and carried him up to the shrine. After half an hour they came down and Swami Aseshananda told the mother, "Please don't worry; he will walk." Later the boy was able to walk. Eventually, the boy became a musician. I heard this story from Mrs. Sheila Gulrajani, a devotee of our Vedanta center in Seattle, to whom Mrs. Freinderich had narrated this incident some years before.

THE STORY OF ONE WHO MISSED AN OPPORTUNITY

In 1958, nearly four months after joining the monastic Order, I got the opportunity to see Swami Premeshananda at the Sargachhi ashrama. A brother monk accompanied me from Shillong.

Swami Premeshananda (1884–1967) was a disciple of the Holy Mother Sri Sarada Devi. At the time of our visit he was in his seventies, and the head of the Sargachhi ashrama. Upon our arrival, we went straight to Swami Premeshananda's room, and found him sitting on his bed in the presence of several devotees. After we saluted the swami, he made kind inquiries of us. Swami Premeshananda asked me, "What's your name?"

I replied, "My name is Brahmachari J…"

He then asked, "What was your name before joining the Order?"

It is not the tradition for monks in India to tell their pre-monastic names to others. So, I hesitated. Observing my hesitation, Swami Premeshananda smilingly said to me, "You needn't hesitate. I am an old monk! You can tell me your pre-monastic name. No harm will come to you."

Then I told him my full premonastic name. My last name, my family surname, was a little bit unusual. Very few families in India had that surname. When I came out of Swami Premeshananda's room, one of the devotees who had been sitting there followed me out. He called me aside, and told me that he had come from Calcutta, and that he was a doctor. Then he added, "I knew a gentleman who had the same surname as yours. When I was studying medicine, he was senior to me in our medical school. I'm still grateful to him, because I got a lot of help from him as a student. I wonder if you are related to him."

When he named that person I understood that he was talking about my elder brother, who was a pathologist in Assam. "I'm his younger brother," I informed the gentleman. He was very pleased to hear that.

He then said to me with great feeling, "While in medical school he treated me almost like his younger brother. I have similar feelings about you. As your well wisher I'm making an ardent request of you: Please promise me that you will never give up monastic life. There is no life greater than this.

"I am a householder now. I have a wife and son. But several years ago I was a brahmachari in the Ramakrishna Order. I joined the Order after getting my medical degree. But after a short while I started noticing defects in the monks. I became restless. The General Secretary was very kind and considerate to me. He let me try three or four different ashramas. But I wasn't happy anywhere. Then one morning, I quietly left the Order and went home.

"My father is a wealthy businessman. He was overjoyed at my return. Lest I change my mind, he arranged for my marriage in great haste. Now that I'm a householder, I realize what a great opportunity I've lost in my spiritual life. A monk's life is a wonderful life. It's a path to inculcate purity, truthfulness and other noble virtues. This path directly leads one to God. But a householder's life is a circuitous path, full of pitfalls, mistakes, and temptations. I know how difficult it is for a householder to make progress in spiritual life.

"I couldn't adjust to monastic life, because I wasn't cut out for that life. I had a secret desire to enjoy the pleasures of family life. That's why I saw imaginary defects in the monks. In order to justify my leaving the Order, my mind concocted negative thoughts about the monks and the monastery. Now I understand these things clearly. But it's too late. I've lost the greatest opportunity of my life. To get some peace of mind, in-between my work, I come here to have the holy company of Swami Premeshananda. Whenever I have a vacation, I try to come here from Calcutta and spend a few days with the swami."

Then he paused for a moment, and continued again, "Family life is a great bondage. One of my friends accompanied me this time from Calcutta. He had heard about the holiness of Swami Premeshananda from me. So he wanted to come with me on this trip to Sargachhi. He was supposed to spend three or four days here, and then return with me to Calcutta. But after spending just one night, he went back. He told me that he missed his wife so much that he couldn't stay here any longer." Then he paused again and said, "I told you that I have a son. He is very young. I wish that he becomes a monk when he grows up."

The doctor, before leaving Sargachhi, reminded me again of his request. About fifteen years later, I went to give a lecture in one of the suburbs of Calcutta. I saw the doctor sitting in the audience. He was in the front row. But he didn't recognize me. After the lecture I saw him leave the hall quickly. I never saw him again.

⧗ LOVE OF THE GURU

SWAMI ATMANANDA
(1868–1923)

Swami Vivekananda had a monastic disciple named Swami Atmananda, also known as Shukul Maharaj. This story is about him. All the junior monks of the Ramakrishna Order respected Swami Atmananda highly because, besides being a disciple of the great Swami Vivekananda, he was also an ideal monk. His lifestyle was very austere. All his life he used the simplest clothes and a hard bed equipped with a blanket, a bed sheet, a pillow, and a mosquito net to protect himself from mosquito bites. Yet during his entire monastic life, no matter in which ashrama he was staying, he would maintain a second bed that he himself never used. Nor would he allow anyone else to use it.

Every morning, with the utmost care, he would make that bed. The bed had a nice mattress, a nice pillow, the cleanest of sheets, and a nice blanket. It also had a mosquito net. Other monks of the ashrama wondered why and for whom Swami Atmananda maintained that second bed. Finally one day, one of the monks asked the swami about it. Then Swami Atmananda explained, "When I was in Belur Math (Belur Monastery), Swamiji (Swami Vivekananda) would sometimes come to my room and lie on my bed. After his passing away, I had a dream about him. I saw that he had come and was lying on my bed. That's why I prepare this second bed for him." While saying this he became choked with emotion and started shedding tears. The monks who were present there were extremely touched by Swami Atmananda's extraordinary love for his guru.

𝕏 OBEDIENCE

A young man named Harendranarayan came to Swami Vijnanananda (1868–1938) and prayed for spiritual initiation. After initiation the swami said to him, "From now on you must practice truthfulness." The young man returned home, but found it extremely hard to practice truthfulness living a worldly life. He was not married, and lived with his parents in a smaller town in West Bengal, not too far from Calcutta. He realized that if he became a monk, he would be able to practice truthfulness without too much difficulty. He left home and became a monk (not of the Ramakrishna Order), assuming the name Brahmachari Harendranarayan. Eventually he started his own ashrama in the city of Cooch Bihar in West Bengal. I heard this story from Brahmachari Harendranarayan himself, when I met him in our Shillong ashrama in 1959.

⧗ THE MYSTERIOUS FRAGRANCE

Two out of the first five years of my monastic life, I spent in the Training Center for novices in Belur Math. On completion of my training, I took my first monastic vows. After the ceremony I was to go back to the Shillong ashrama.

During my stay in Belur Math, every morning I and the other monks went to salute Swami Sankarananda (1880–1961), who was then the President of the Ramakrishna Order. His room was on the second floor of the original monastery building. As soon as we would climb the staircase leading to Swami Sankarananda's room, we would smell the fine fragrance of incense coming from the swami's room. Entering his room was like entering a holy shrine permeated by a very fine fragrance of incense. The fragrance was so sweet that I often wondered which brand of incense was used for Swami Sankarananda's room.

When the time for my return to the Shillong ashrama drew near, I went to Brahmachari "N" who was the chief attendant to Swami Sankarananda and asked, "Will you please tell me what brand of incense you use for Swami Sankarananda's room? I would like to buy some and take it back to our Shillong ashrama."

Brahmachari "N" named a common brand of incense. I said to him, "I know that brand well. But the fragrance from the incense in Swami Sankarananda's room is very different, and so much sweeter."

Brahmachari "N" said, "I'm going to tell you a secret. I haven't told this to anyone except for one or two devotees."

"What's the secret?" I asked.

Brahmachari "N" confided, "It's not the fragrance of the incense you're smelling. It comes out of Swami Sankarananda's body. The fragrance comes from his body."

I asked, "Is this true?"

Brahmachari "N" replied, "It's 100% true. Not only his body, but even his T-shirt emits that fragrance. The cloth he wears, and the wrapper he uses—all have that smell. Even after washing some of it remains."

I didn't want to disbelieve Brahmachari "N." I knew that it was not impossible for great yogis to give off that kind of fragrance from their bodies. But the tradition of the Ramakrishna Order is very different. The personified spiritual ideal of our Order, Sri Ramakrishna, always spoke against using occult powers, as did Sri Krishna and Gautama Buddha. I never heard that Sri Ramakrishna's body had emitted any sweet fragrance. Nor did I ever hear that the bodies of any of his disciples had given off fragrance. How could it have been possible that Swami Sankarananda alone was an exception to our Order's tradition of not using occult powers?

I thought it best to get a second opinion. I went to another attendant of Swami Sankarananda, and asked him about the mysterious fragrance.

He said to me, "Brahmachari "N" doesn't know the secret. Swami Sankarananda is very austere. He doesn't want to use mosquito nets at night. So every evening we spray a mosquito repellant called Nipo, made by Calcutta Chemical Company. We spray until the last mosquito in his room is either gone or dies. Then we shut the windows of his room to keep out other mosquitoes. It's the smell of Nipo, combined with the smell of incense that creates that sweet fragrance. Since the room is permeated with the fine vapor of Nipo, the smell even penetrates his clothes and adds a sweet fragrance to them."

This is how the mystery of the sweet fragrance in Swami Sankarananda's room was solved. This incident shows that if we draw conclusions without rational investigation, many natural events may easily be hailed as miracles.

SOME REMINISCENCES ABOUT SWAMI SHANTANANDA

SWAMI SHANTANANDA
(1884–1974)

Swami Shantananda was one of the early disciples of the Holy Mother Sri Sarada Devi. Monks of the Ramakrishna Order respected him as a highly evolved spiritual soul. When I saw him first in Belur Math, he was already an elderly monk in his late seventies. He lived in a small room on the first floor of the Premananda Memorial Building. He suffered from different old age ailments, so there was an attendant to take care of him. His attendant, a younger swami, lived in the adjoining room.

Swami Shantananda was very gentle by nature and usually reticent. Even though he wouldn't speak much, his saintliness attracted many devotees. Some came to see him every day. In the afternoon, he would sit in his chair and quietly listen to one or another holy book being read out to him. He was particularly fond of *The Gospel of Sri Ramakrishna*. It was usually this book that would be read every day. Having read the book many times in his life, he had got the entire book by heart. Whenever the reader would make any mistake, the swami would gently correct him.

One day during the reading of the *Gospel*, the topic of the *anahata dhwani* or the *music of the spheres* came up. It is the mystical sound that only a yogi can hear with his inner spiritual ear. In the *Gospel* Sri Ramakrishna was saying, "There is *Shabda-Brahman* (Brahman that is identical with the anahata sound). The sages perform spiritual austerities to hear that sound. The sound of the anahata rises spontaneously from the navel. Those who are spiritually illumined can hear this sound."

Other than the devotee who was reading the *Gospel*, there were three or four other devotees present in the swami's room. One of them commented, "The ancient sages who were spiritually illumined heard that anahata sound. But does anyone today hear it?"

Swami Shantananda, who rarely spoke about his own spiritual experiences, suddenly broke his silence and said gently, "Yes, one can hear that sound, I'm hearing that sound right now."

One gentleman I knew developed a genuine yearning for spiritual life. He used to visit Belur Math every day without fail. He would come, salute the deities in the temples, and then go and see Swami Shantananda, whom he respected highly. Before going home he would sometimes come and see me in the headquarters office. One day he said to me, "Maharaj, I would like to have diksha (spiritual initiation)."

I said, "Please go to our President's office. It's only our President, Swami Vireswarananda, who gives spiritual initiation here. But first you have to talk to the swami who is his private secretary. He will arrange for your diksha."

The gentleman then went to the private secretary of Swami Vireswarananda. The swami gave him a form to be filled out. The purpose of the form was to collect some personal information about the candidate praying for diksha. But the very idea of a form turned him off. The gentleman had expected to get an appointment to talk with Swami Vireswarananda first. He wanted to have some personal contact with Swami Vireswarananda before receiving diksha.

He came back and told me frankly what had happened. He was not sure if he would go again to Swami Vireswarananda's office for diksha.

I told him, "That little formality shouldn't turn you off. Swami Vireswarananda is very elderly, and there are many candidates for diksha. It would be a great strain on him if he had to give personal interviews to each and every candidate for diksha. To relieve him of that strain, the form is used. Swami Vireswarananda carefully goes through each and every form, and decides whom he wants to initiate. Being very compassionate, he usually grants the prayers of just about all the candidates. So I advise you to go again to Swami Vireswarananda's office."

But the gentleman was still reluctant. He then went to Swami Shantananda's room to salute him. It is interesting that although the gentleman had gone to see Swami Shantananda many times before, the swami had never spoken to him. But on that particular day, he suddenly asked that gentleman, "Have you had diksha?"

The gentleman replied, "No, Maharaj."

Swami Shantananda said, "You should have diksha."

The gentleman, with great eagerness, asked, "Will you please give me diksha?"

Swami Shantananda replied, "I don't give diksha. Please go to Prabhu Maharaj. He will give you diksha." (Swami Vireswarananda was also called Prabhu Maharaj.)

The gentleman saluted Swami Shantananda and straight-away came back to me. He was crying. In a choked voice he said to me, "Swami Shantananda has shattered my stubborn ego." Then with tears in his eyes, he told me what had happened between him and Swami Shantananda.

He approached Swami Vireswarananda again and was blessed by diksha.

One may wonder why Swami Shantananda, who hadn't spoken a single word to that gentleman in all those days, would suddenly ask him about his diksha. Was he a thought-reader? Did he use occult power? To my understanding, he would never use such powers. Sri Ramakrishna, the Divine Incarnation, sometimes uses pure souls as conduits to shower His grace on devotees. Swami Shantananda was such a pure conduit. The words that came out of his mouth were no other than the words of Sri Ramakrishna.

⧗ HOLINESS ALWAYS WINS

Swami Saradeswarananda was the head of our Kamarpukur ashrama, and had been for many years. Kamarpukur was the birthplace of Sri Ramakrishna. One afternoon a gentleman came to see Swami Saradeswarananda. He said, "I want to stay as a guest in your ashrama for two or three days."

The policy of the Ramakrishna Order is not to allow strangers to come and stay as ashrama guests. Anyone seeking accommodation as a guest is expected to carry a letter of introduction from a swami of the Ramakrishna Order. So Swami Saradeswarananda asked, "Do you have a letter of introduction from any of our swamis?"

"No." replied the stranger.

Swami Saradeswarananda then said, "We're sorry. Without a letter of introduction, we can't accommodate anyone as a guest in our ashrama."

The words of Swami Saradeswarananda enraged the stranger. He raised his voice and shouted profanities at the swami for several minutes. Some devotees and monks of the ashrama were present. They found the stranger's insulting words to the elderly swami intolerable. But Swami Saradeswarananda remained completely calm and unperturbed. After the ravings of the stranger ceased, Swami Saradeswarananda gently said to a monk, "Give this gentleman some prasad (food that has been offered to God)." The stranger wouldn't accept the prasad. He immediately left.

Next morning the stranger returned and went up to Swami Saradeswarananda, who was sitting on a chair, and fell flat at his feet. Then he sat up, and with his hands folded in the gesture of salutation said, "Maharaj, I'm a gangster from Calcutta." (He was a very notorious gangster of greater Calcutta, and well known throughout the state of West Bengal. But none at the ashrama had ever met him before.)

"One of your neighbors is antagonistic to your ashrama. He hired me to insult you. That's why I behaved with you in that insulting manner. You must be a great saint. The foul language that I used would have enraged anyone, but you remained completely unaffected. Please bless and forgive me."

The swami comforted the gangster and asked him to stay for lunch. But the man replied, "If you permit, in the future I'll come again along with my wife. When we come, will you kindly allow us to stay in this holy ashrama for a day or two?" The swami nodded his consent.

Later the gangster came back with his wife, and stayed in the ashrama guesthouse for a few days. During his visit, the gangster would sit in the temple every morning after taking his bath, and would chant from memory many hymns from *Sri Sri Chandi.* His devotion to God surprised the monks and devotees of the ashrama.

THE EFFECT OF BAD KARMA

According to the doctrine of karma, good actions produce good effects, bad actions bad. The effects of some actions immediately come to us. For example, if I put my hand into fire, it will immediately be burnt. In this case the effect of my action comes back to me immediately. But some actions have late-bearing effects. If I sow an apple seed, it will take years for the apple tree to grow and yield fruits. In this case, the effect of my action comes to me much later. The effects of some late-bearing actions may not show up until our next incarnation. But the Hindu scriptures say that the effect of *atyutkata karma* (a hideous or ghastly action) comes back to the doer in this very life. Nobody can escape it. Killing or tormenting a holy person, killing a woman, etc. are examples of atyutkata karma.

We had an elderly swami who was the head of one of our

ashramas in West Bengal. The swami was very gentle in nature. But he was often hassled by a neighbor. The neighbor was very ill-tempered, and frequently used minor excuses to verbally abuse the swami. It was not in the nature of the swami to quarrel with anybody. In spite of frequent provocations, he always remained unaffected and calm. This made the neighbor all the more abusive. One day, in a fit of violent rage, he came to the elderly swami and gave him a slap. Such behavior is unthinkable in Indian tradition. But the swami said or did nothing. He quietly endured the insult.

Much later I had to go to that ashrama in connection with flood relief work being conducted by the monks there. This was my first visit to the ashrama. The elderly swami was no longer there. He had passed away many years before. I was accommodated in a room on the second floor of the residential building.

One day as I looked out the window of my room, I noticed the courtyard of the neighbor's home. I saw there a very dark complexioned old man, extremely thin, and all bent over. He looked like a frightening apparition. Only his left arm was normal. His right arm was bent and withered like the dry branch of a tree. It hung loosely down on one side of his body. That strange-looking person was slowly collecting fallen leaves from the ground with his left hand.

Later I asked our monks who the old man was. I was told: "He is the man who slapped our swami with his right hand, many years ago. Shortly after slapping the swami his right arm started getting paralyzed. Eventually, it became completely emaciated and withered away like a dry twig. We've heard that he went to all kinds of doctors, but no one could help him."

Here was an example of the effect of atyutkata karma. The wrongdoer couldn't escape the inexorable law of karma. It came back to punish him with full force.

🏺 HOW TO COMFORT THE BEREAVED

A swami in his early forties was made the head of our ashrama in New Delhi. The ashrama had many devotees. Occasionally some of them would lose their near and dear ones, and come to the swami seeking comfort. But the swami felt unable to provide it. He realized that words, no matter how sympathetic, could not comfort a woman who had lost her only child.

The swami had great respect for an elderly and saintly monk of our Order named Swami Saradeshananda (1895–1989), who lived in our Vrindaban ashrama. This elderly swami was a disciple of the Holy Mother Sri Sarada Devi. The city of Vrindaban is not far from New Delhi. On one occasion when the swami of the New Delhi Ashrama went to see Swami Saradeshananda in Vrindaban he asked Swami Saradeshananda, "Maharaj, how should I comfort a grief-stricken person when he or she comes to me for comfort? I'm at a loss to know how any words of mine can possibly comfort them. I feel completely inadequate."

Swami Saradeshananda replied, "You don't have to say anything. During all these years of your monastic life, you must have found some inner peace. When bereaved people come to you, they will benefit from the peaceful state of your mind. Just by being in your presence their minds will gradually become calm and peaceful."

⧗ A RAMAKRISHNA TRADITION

This incident happened during the first one or two months of my joining the Ramakrishna Order. At that time, I was under the impression that meditation and the study of the scriptures was superior to the other activities of the ashrama. One morning, during a religious festival, the monks and devotees of the ashrama were singing devotional songs to the accompaniment of drums, cymbals, and the harmonium in the temple. I stayed in the temple for a little while, but the thought came to my mind that rather than singing, it was better for me to go to my room and either meditate, or quietly read some holy book. So I returned to my room, picked out a holy book, and began reading it at my desk. A few minutes later Swami Krishnatmananda (1906–1996), the manager of the ashrama, entered my room. He was in his sixties then. He asked, "Why are you sitting here alone? Others are having such joy singing in the temple!"

I replied, "Maharaj, I don't find much joy in singing that way. Group singing disturbs me. The quick rhythm of the music makes my mind agitated. I feel much better reading a holy book or trying to meditate quietly in my room."

Swami Krishnatmananda said, "But this is not the tradition of our Order. We have to be in *jhal* (a spicy hot curry), *jhol* (a bland soup), and *ambal* (a sweet and sour dish). We're not supposed to be monotonous." Then he left my room.

Swami Krishnatmananda was an exemplary monk. I had great respect for him. His words made me think. A little self-examination revealed that, unknown to myself, I had been pampering my ego with a false sense of superiority. I considered myself superior to others, because I preferred meditation.

My self-examination also made me realize that the monks and devotees were happy singing in the temple for a very special reason. They were singing for the pleasure of the Deity. Their songs were an offering to God. I hurried back to the temple and wholeheartedly joined in the singing.

⧗ WASTED ADVICE

I had a friend named Subodh Baral. He was a devotee of Sri Ramakrishna, and used to frequently visit the local Ramakrishna ashrama. He told me this story:

One day, accompanied by a friend, he went to the ashrama for a visit. While sitting in the living room (drawing room), they started discussing various topics. When they came to the topic of how to improve themselves spiritually, there was a difference of opinion between the two. Subodh's friend said that nothing worthwhile could be achieved through spiritual progress alone. What was more important in life was to achieve worldly success by hard work and the right kind of motivation. Subodh Baral thought differently. Being a devotee, he thought that spiritual progress was the most beneficial thing in human life. As they had two conflicting opinions, they started arguing with each other. The debate continued for nearly an hour. Then the friend left.

A swami was in an adjoining room. He overheard the entire conversation. He came out of his room and said to Subodh, "Excuse me for listening to your conversation. It was indeed interesting. But I noticed that for about an hour you were trying to advise a person who was determined not to listen to your advice. As I see it, both of you only wasted your time."

Subodh Baral was deeply impressed by the swami's words.

He realized that the swami was right. From then on he stopped giving unnecessary advice to people.

⧗ THE SECRET OF SERVICE

SWAMI SAUMYANANDA
(1895–1977)

After I joined the Ramakrishna ashrama in Shillong as a novice, I had the good fortune to spend a few years with Swami Saumyananda, the head of the ashrama. The swami was nearly seventy years old at that time. He was an exemplary monk and endowed with wonderful qualities, and I developed great respect for him. He had a winning smile that radiated purity and love.

One of my first duties at the ashrama was to help in the kitchen. Swami Saumyananda had a defunct gall bladder, and had been advised by his physician to eat a fat-free diet. I used to prepare his special food in a steam cooker (something like a pressure cooker) and would serve his meals in his room.

The paid sweeper wouldn't do a satisfactory job of cleaning our toilets, so we younger monks took upon ourselves the duty of cleaning the bathrooms. We did such a good job that the toilet bowls and the floors of the bathrooms were always sparklingly clean.

After using the toilet, one could flush it by pulling a handle attached to a small tank of water hung from the ceiling. Due to faulty plumbing, however, the tanks always dripped water. So they weren't used. Instead, a bucket would be filled with water from a tap inside the bathroom and poured into the toilet bowl to flush it clean. The buckets were made of galvanized steel. But, in time, some of them lost their protective coating and rusted.

We were taught that everything in the ashrama belonged to Sri Ramakrishna. Every object in the ashrama was to be handled with care. Nothing was to be wasted. After the toilets were used, the buckets were often left partially filled with water. But I thought that when not in use, they should be kept empty and dry. That would protect them from rusting. So, every time I used the bathroom, I would make sure that I left the bucket completely dry. In order to be doubly sure, I would leave the bucket upside down.

Once, when I was serving the midday meal to Swami Saumyananda, he said to me, "This morning I used the bathroom immediately after you used it. I noticed that you left the bucket upside down. May I know why you did that?"

I replied, "Everything in the ashrama, including the buckets, belongs to Sri Ramakrishna. We are supposed to make sure that no harm comes to anything. To prevent the rusting of the buckets in the bathroom, I put them upside down in order to drain out the last drops of water."

Swami Saumyananda said, "Your attitude is the right attitude. But I'll teach you one thing. We've come to the monastery to give service to others, looking upon them as the veritable manifestations of God. But the monks with whom we live are usually very reluctant to accept personal service from anyone.

So I'll teach you how to serve others without even letting them know that you've served them. After using the bathroom, mop the floor as you normally do, and then leave a bucket full of water. The monk who comes after you to use the bathroom will find a clean bathroom, and will have to use that water collected by you. That'll be your silent service to him."

Swami Saumyananda is no more, but his teaching has found a permanent place in my heart. It has inspired me to give, wherever possible, that kind of service that craves no recognition.

⧗ A MYSTERIOUS INCIDENT CONNECTED TO THE PRACTICE OF KARMA YOGA

Swami Vishwarupananda (1901–1975), also known as Ramgati Maharaj, was for many years attached to the Ramakrishna Mission Home of Service in Varanasi. The Home of Service is a charitable hospital run by the Ramakrishna Order. In those days, in addition to administrative work, the monks had to work in the hospital doing nursing, cleaning, dressing of wounds (bandaging), etc. Following the tradition established by Swami Vivekananda, they all tried to serve the patients looking upon them as the veritable manifestations of God.

Swami Vishwarupananda, then a young monk, was asked to work in the "dressing room" of the hospital, where wounds are cleaned and bandaged. The swami had been trained to clean and bandage the wounds of patients. The vast majority of such patients came from poverty-stricken neighborhoods in the city and nearby villages. There were no antibiotics in those days, and wounds took a much longer time to heal. Often many turned septic and malodorous. The swami was very sensitive to bad odors. Though he considered it a great privilege to serve these patients, his sensitivity to odors made it extremely difficult for him to work there. The odors from some wounds were so bad that they made him nauseous. As a result, he often lost his appetite and couldn't eat. Nevertheless, he didn't want to switch to any other duty. He felt that it was a great opportunity for him to serve those patients suffering from festering wounds.

SWAMI SARADANANDA
(1865–1927)

Around this time, Swami Saradananda, a spiritually exalted disciple of Sri Ramakrishna and Swami Vishwarupananda's guru, visited the Varanasi sevashrama. Swami Vishwarupananda took this opportunity to speak with his guru about his problem and Swami Saradananda asked him to pray to Sri Ramakrishna for help. The next day, when Swami Vishwarupananda went to the dressing room of the hospital to work, to his utter surprise he could no longer smell the festering wounds that he had to clean and bandage. From then onwards he had no more difficulty dressing wounds.

Often florists who handle fragrant flowers all the time gradually lose their sense of smell. Did something similar happen to Swami Vishwarupananda? It doesn't seem probable. He lost his sense of smell suddenly after his prayer to Sri Ramakrishna. It didn't happen gradually. How to explain this? Was it the power of prayer that made it happen? Or was it something else?

⧖ SWAMI ADINATHANANDA'S UNIQUE METHODS OF TRAINING JUNIOR MONKS

SWAMI ADINATHANANDA
(1902–1995)

Swami Adinathananda, also known in the Ramakrishna Order as Kali Da, was a disciple of the Holy Mother Sri Sarada Devi. He spent most of his monastic life being involved in the educational activities of our Order. For many years he was the head of our ashrama in the city of Jamshedpur in India. The ashrama ran eleven excellent schools in the city.

Other than the swamis, there were three or four brahmacharis in the ashrama. One of the brahmacharis was Sukdeb. One of his responsibilities was to clean Swami Adinathananda's room. He would sweep the swami's room, dust the furniture, and sometimes change the bed sheets. One day while changing the sheets, Sukdeb saw something drop to the floor from under the mattress. It was Swami Adinathananda's diary. The diary was lying open on the floor. Sukdeb could not help noticing his own name written on the open page of the diary. Curious, he read what Swami Adinathananda had written about him. Interestingly the date written on the page was a day that was yet to come. Swami Adinathananda had written, "Today I've to scold Sukdeb."

This surprised Sukdeb. Swami Adinathananda would occasionally scold the junior monks, pointing out their defects. But Sukdeb never imagined that the swami planned in advance when to scold a monk! Scolding is a part of the disciplining in the Ramakrishna Order. The official name of our Order is the Ramakrishna Mission. Some of our senior monks humorously call it the *Ramakrishna Machine.* What kind of machine? An ego-crushing machine! When monks join the Order they bring along with them all the sharp corners and angularities in their characters. But as soon as they enter the ego-crushing machine, the grinding process starts. When the grinding process is over, the finished products are highly polished, well-rounded personalities that are fit to serve the Order!

Swami Adinathananda knew that his scolding would help crush the false egos of the junior monks. That's why he would plan in advance whom to scold and when. For him it was nothing but playacting. His scolding was an expression of his genuine love and goodwill for his junior brother monks.

Another incident. Brahmachari Uggappa was then the cashier of the Jamshedpur ashrama. The ashrama used to get grants from the government to run its schools. The checks for such grants would come to the ashrama at different periods of time throughout the year. Once a check for a substantial amount came from the government. But it arrived late on a Saturday afternoon, after the banks were closed. The next morning Swami Adinathananda told Uggappa, "Go to the bank and deposit the check."

Uggappa replied, "Maharaj, it's Sunday today. The bank is closed. It's impossible to deposit the check today."

Swami Adinathananda said, "You haven't even tried to deposit it, and you're saying that it's impossible! First go and try. Then come and tell me that you couldn't deposit the check!"

Uggappa knew that it was impossible for him to deposit the check that day, because the bank was closed. Nevertheless, he decided to give it a try. The ashrama was an important client of the bank, and the officer in charge of the bank knew Swami Adinathananda well. Besides that, the swami was well known in the city, and highly respected by one and all. Uggappa straightaway went to the officer's home. The officer received him cordially. Uggappa then told him what Swami Adinathananda had said. Hearing that, the officer pondered for a few moments and said to Uggappa, "Let's go to the bank. Let me see what I can do for you!" Then they both went to the bank. The officer unlocked the front door of the bank, took the check from Uggappa, entered the cashier's office and deposited the check in the ashrama's account.

Uggappa returned to the ashrama and told Swami Adinathananda what had happened. Swami Adinathananda said, "Now you've learnt that if we try, what seems to be impossible, can become possible."

Another word about Swami Adinathananda. He was a great karma yogi. His exemplary, loving, and well-rounded personality was the outcome of his practice of karma yoga. Once he said, "By Sri Ramakrishna's grace, I have been able to burn my animal passions through work." The work he referred to was the selfless service that he had given throughout his monastic life to the Order.

Part II

⌛ BON BABA—A GREAT KARMA-YOGI

SWAMI MUKTANANDA
(BONBIHARI MAHARAJ)
(1903–1996)

His name was Swami Muktananda, but most of the monks of the Ramakrishna Order knew him as Bonbihari Maharaj. Almost all his monastic life he was attached to our hospital center in Varanasi, known as the Ramakrishna Mission Home of Service. Those people of Varanasi who at one time or another had been treated at our hospital, remembered him fondly and called him Bon Baba, meaning Holy Man Bon or Father Bon. He worked in the surgical department of the hospital, where he bandaged wounds, surgical or otherwise. He worked there day after day, year after year, with the greatest dedication possible. As a result, he developed an extraordinary ability to predict how soon wounds would heal just by looking at them. He was so skilled in his work that the wounds he dressed healed faster than those dressed by others. Some surgeons agreed to perform complicated surgery only on condition that Bon Baba would take charge of the postoperative care of the patient.

When I saw him first at the Varanasi hospital, nearly forty-three years ago, he was most probably in his fifties. He was quite strong physically. He had a winning smile that revealed his childlike simplicity. He was an untiring worker, always ready to serve patients in the right spirit of karma yoga.

At all odd hours, often at midnight, patients would be brought to the emergency ward of the hospital, and without the slightest sign of displeasure, he would immediately go and take care of them. Many days he hardly had any time to sleep. But I never saw him upset over it.

Bonbihari Maharaj was also extremely fond of visiting the temple of Lord Viswanath (Shiva). Every day, very early in the morning, whether it was in the extreme cold of winter or the tortuous heat of summer, he walked nearly a mile from the ashrama to bathe in the river Ganga, and then went to the temple to offer his worship there. In old age he developed arthritis in his knees, but that didn't deter him from following this daily routine until he became partially wheelchair bound toward the end of his life.

Even when he was almost unable to walk, he would go to the hospital and help dress the wounds of patients. A brahmachari or helper would take him from the monastery to the hospital by wheelchair, and he would joyfully serve the patients, looking upon them as the veritable manifestations of God.

It is often seen that those who work for a long time in a hospital as a nurse or doctor are no longer emotionally affected by the deaths of patients. But Bon Baba never lost the sensitivity of his heart. He had great sympathy for the bereaved families of patients. Our scriptures say that anyone who dies in Varanasi becomes liberated by Lord Shiva's grace. This belief must have given him some comfort when he saw patients die at our hospital. In addition to his great dedication in serving patients, it was his loving and compassionate heart that endeared him to all who came in contact with him.

Like other swamis of the Ramakrishna Order, he also had a keen sense of humor. Once he told me a true and very humorous story. In connection with the story it is necessary to mention that our hospital in Varanasi has a large dairy with a fair number of milk cows. The milk from the dairy is mainly used for the patients in the hospital. Occasionally, someone has to go to the villages and buy fodder for the cows. Once Bon Baba had to go to a village to buy fodder. He had to go quite a few miles by train. When his train finally arrived at the village, the merchant who was to supply the fodder came to receive the swami at the railroad station. The swami was also expected to stay overnight in the merchant's home as his guest. From now on I shall record the rest of the story as told by Bon Baba:

He said, "The merchant's home was close to the railroad station. We both started walking down the dirt road, lined on both sides by the modest homes of the villagers. Then we arrived at a very large and impressive-looking house. I asked the merchant, 'Whose home is this?'

"Folding his hands in a gesture of salutation, the merchant very humbly replied, 'Revered sir, this is your home!' By that I understood that it was his home. (In India, to express great humility and a spirit of submission, some people talk like that to holy men.)

"Then we entered the living room of the house. There were several children of different ages in the living room. One by one they saluted me. I asked the merchant, 'Who are these children?'

"The merchant replied with great humility, 'They are yours, revered sir.' I understood that they were his children.

"About this time a lady, apparently his wife, entered the living room and saluted me. I didn't dare ask the merchant who she was!"

⧗ FUN AND HUMOR IN MONASTIC LIFE

The Mukherjee family was the next-door neighbors of our ashrama in Shillong. One evening, while we, the monks of the ashrama, were having dinner, Mr. Mukherjee suddenly appeared unannounced at the door of our dining room. Swami Saumyananda, the head of the ashrama, asked, "What's the matter Mr. Mukherjee? What brings you here this evening?"

Mr. Mukherjee replied, "Maharaj, please forgive me for this untimely interruption. I've come here because I had an argument with my wife about something. Your dining room is just a few feet away from ours. Every time you have lunch or dinner, we hear peals of laughter coming from your dining room. My wife says, 'The monks must be eating very well. They must eat delicacies every day. That's why they are so happy.'

"But I told her, 'The ashrama is poor. How can the monks get to eat delicacies?' This is why I've come to see what you're eating."

Swami Saumyananda said, "Please sit down and join us for supper. Then you'll have firsthand experience of what we eat!"

But Mr. Mukherjee didn't sit down and eat with us. He just stood and watched what we were eating. Our dinner consisted of rice, dal (lentils), and a simple vegetable dish. That's all. An average middle-class family of India would consider that meal extremely simple. And we ate the same dishes day after day. With a winning smile on his face, Mr. Mukherjee then headed home. From then onwards, Mr. Mukherjee off and on would bring some sweetmeats prepared by his wife to our temple. The purpose was to occasionally provide the monks with something tastier than their usual monotonous food.

CHARLES MATHIAS

Those not acquainted with monastic life in India may think that a monk's life must be totally devoid of fun and humor. This notion does not apply to the monks of the Ramakrishna Order. Sri Ramakrishna once said to the Divine Mother, "Mother, please don't make me a monk whose heart is dry and devoid of a sense of humor. Allow me to enjoy humor with due restraint." Humor is often used to harm and ridicule people. The Ramakrishna monks restrain themselves from indulging in that kind of humor. The humor used in Ramakrishna monasteries is totally innocent and harmless. When the monks meet in the dining hall, they tell funny stories or jokes that cause great joy and fun.

The monks occasionally indulge in mimicry and practical jokes as well. Swami Shivananda, one of those great saintly disciples of Sri Ramakrishna, was for many years the President of our Order. He enjoyed mimicry. He would sometimes ask a junior monk who was good at mimicry, to perform in his presence. Sri Ramakrishna himself was a very good mimic. In one place in *The Gospel of Sri Ramakrishna* we read: "Sri Ramakrishna was seated on the small couch in his room and enjoying the company of some pure-minded devotees. He started humoring them by mimicking the mannerisms of professional women singers of Bengal. Seeing his wonderful mimicry the devotees started laughing aloud."

God-realized souls have a natural tendency to commune with God. It is hard for them to bring their minds down to the worldly level. But compassion for those who are suffering from a lack of spirituality sometimes drags their minds to this level. This was very true for the spiritually illumined disciples of Sri Ramakrishna. For example, Swami Brahmananda would try to bring his mind down by playfully trying to catch fish (even though he was reportedly not at all good at fishing). Swami Akhandananda would sometimes try to bring his mind down by playing cards with the junior monks. Some would also take recourse to doing humorous things. Swami Shivaswarupananda, then a junior monk in Belur Math (Monastery), witnessed the following funny incident associated with Swami Akhandananda:

At Belur Math the monks usually have their lunch or supper sitting in two batches, one after the other. The majority of the monks eat in the first batch. Monks who serve the meal for the first batch usually eat in the second. This following incident happened when Swami Akhandananda (1864–1937) had come to Belur Math for a visit from the Sargachhi ashrama.

One evening he invited four or five junior monks to join him at supper in the second batch. Swami Shivaswarupananda was one of them. When the monks arrived at the dining hall, Swami Akhandananda announced that he had decided to celebrate the birthday of King George the Fifth of England that evening by enjoying a special meal. There were two or three extra dishes, in addition to the usual lentil and vegetable dishes served every evening.

Swami Akhandananda had no idea whatsoever of when King George the Fifth was born. Aside from that, the Indians were at that time engaged in their struggle for freedom from British rule. In short, they had no love for the British monarch.

When the meal was over, Swami Akhandananda said to Swami Shivaswarupananda, "Say, 'Victory to King George the Fifth.'" But the younger swami was reluctant to obey Swami Akhandananda. Instead, he said, "Victory to Sri Ramakrishna!" and immediately got up from his seat. The incident caused a lot of laughter.

We had a monk in our Order named Swami Yogiswarananda, also known as Upu Da (Big Brother Upu). He was a disciple of Swami Brahmananda, and spent most of his monastic life in Belur Math. Swami Abhayananda, the manager of Belur Math, once played a practical joke on Swami Yogiswarananda. It was the rainy season. During that season, thousands of little, young frogs could be seen crawling all over the lawns of Belur Math. Belur Math

SWAMI ABHAYANANDA
(1889–1989)

is situated on the river Ganga, and these frogs come crawling up from the river.

Swami Abhayananda obtained an empty container that had once contained *rasagollas,* a favorite sweetmeat of Bengal, and asked someone to fill it with the young frogs. Then it was put on Swami Yogiswarananda's bed after he had gone out for a walk. As soon as he returned, Swami Abhayananda said to Swami Yogiswarananda, "Go to your room. We've put something for you on your bed."

Swami Yogiswarananda went to his room and was happy to see the container of rasagollas on his bed. But to his surprise, when he opened the container, all those frogs leaped out at him.

Another incident. There was a swami named Rajen Maharaj in our hospital center in Varanasi. He was completely bald. To tease him, a brother monk named Indreswar secretly mail-ordered a bottle of hair dye for the swami. The company sent the parcel by C.O.D.— to be paid for in cash on delivery.

When the parcel arrived, the cashier of the ashrama paid the mailman without knowing what the parcel contained, and then charged Rajen Maharaj for it. The swami was amazed to get the parcel, because he had never ordered it. Nevertheless, he had to pay the cashier. Monks of the Ramakrishna Order don't get allowances. Once in a great while devotees may give small sums of money to the monks as gifts. Rajen Maharaj had received a very small sum of money that way, and he used that money to pay the cashier.

As soon as he opened the parcel, Rajen Maharaj realized that he was the victim of a prank. The novel idea of ordering a bottle of hair dye for Rajen Maharaj, who was completely bald, caused a lot of laughter in the ashrama. But Rajen Maharaj, for obvious reasons, didn't heartily join in.

Now I'll tell you another funny incident about the same Rajen Maharaj. It happened in the same hospital center of the Ramakrishna Order in Varanasi.

Nearly seventy years ago life in Belur Math was very austere. For want of funds, only the simplest food could be given to the resident monks. In those days Belur Math, and the areas surrounding it, were infested with mosquitoes. The only source of drinking water for the monks was the heavily silted and polluted water of the river Ganga. As a result, the monks suffered from repeated attacks of dysentery, diarrhea, and malaria. There were virtually no facilities for treatment of the ailing monks.

It was, and still is, the policy of the Ramakrishna Order that all its branches have to be financially self-sufficient. Thus some of the branches are relatively affluent, while others are poor. The standard of living at the hospital center in Varanasi was much better than that of Belur Math. As it was a hospital center, medical treatment was also easily available to the monks there.

Rajen Maharaj had been at that center for many years, and he loved the holy city of Varanasi. He dreaded the possibility of being transferred to Belur Math, mainly due to his love of Varanasi, and partly because of the austere life there. He often expressed his desire never to leave Varanasi. His desire never to leave Varanasi gave some of his brother monks the idea of playing a practical joke on him.

They took a certain devotee into their confidence. The devotee held an executive position, and had his own orderly. The monks procured a telegraph form from the post office and printed a false message on it, supposedly from the headquarters. The fake telegram was addressed to the head of the Varanasi hospital center. It read, "Send Rajen immediately to Belur Math." The orderly, masquerading as a postman, delivered the telegram to Swami Asimananda, the head of the hospital center.

After receiving the telegram, Swami Asimananda called Rajen Maharaj and told him that he would have to go to Belur Math. This scared Rajen Maharaj very much, and almost tearfully he said to Swami Asimananda, "Why me? What wrong have I done? Why are the authorities transferring me to Belur Math?" Seeing his terribly upset condition, the brother monks who had engineered the prank realized that the joke had gone too far. They came to Swami Asimananda and told him frankly what they had done.

Swami Asimananda found the incident very amusing. Then he called Rajen Maharaj and told him that he wouldn't have to go to Belur Math. This information relieved Rajen Maharaj of his anxiety, and a big smile appeared on his face.

⧗ THE DOGS OF BELUR MATH

Among the disciples of Sri Ramakrishna, Swami Vivekananda (1863–1902) and Swami Shivananda (1854–1937) were especially fond of pets. Swami Vivekananda had two pet goats named Hanshi and Motru, a pet antelope, a pet stork, and some ducks and geese. Swami Shivananda had two pet dogs, named Kelo and Bhulo. During the time of Swami Vivekananda, there were three dogs in Belur Math—Bagha, Lily and Mary. But it was Bagha that was known as Swami Vivekananda's dog.

CHARLES MATHIAS

Bagha had been a stray mongrel. As a puppy he had been picked up from the street by Haru Thakur, the cook of Belur Math (Belur Monastery). The monks grew fond of the dog. As Swami Vivekananda was also fond of Bagha, others started calling it Swami Vivekananda's dog.

Once Bagha defecated in front of the shrine. This upset the monks very much. It was decided that the dog should be sent elsewhere. Accordingly, someone took the dog by boat to the other bank of the river Ganga, which flows by Belur Math, and released him there. But Bagha jumped back on the boat and wouldn't leave until the boatmen brought him back to Belur Math. That entire day Bagha hid himself from the residents of the monastery.

Swami Vivekananda's room was on the second floor of the monastery building. The bathroom he used was also on the second floor, but was not attached to his room. There were two staircases going up to the second floor. One of them was outside the building, and was usually used by the sweeper who cleaned the upstairs bathroom.

The day after Bagha was brought back from the other bank of the river, Swami Vivekananda went to his bathroom in the early hours of the morning. It was still dark outside. Bagha had come up to the second floor by the outside staircase, and was lying near the entrance to the bathroom. It was dark and Swami Vivekananda couldn't see him clearly. As he was about to step on Bagha, the dog started whimpering and rubbing his head against Swami Vivekananda's feet as if to complain about what the swami's brother monks had tried to do to him. It is strange that Bagha had never before gone upstairs, nor did he ever go again. This was the one and only time he did.

Later that morning Swami Vivekananda said to the other monks, "Bagha thinks that I am the boss here. That's why he came to me to complain in the early hours of the morning. You needn't punish him for what he did in front of the shrine."

As mentioned earlier, Belur Math had two other dogs, Lily and Mary. They were females. Bagha's nature was completely different from them. Dogs usually have a pecking order. When food is given to them, it is the lead dog that goes and eats first. Although Bagha was the lead dog in the pack, he was never the first to go and eat. He always allowed Lily and Mary to eat first. This surprised the Belur Math monks, because it was quite unlike usual canine behavior.

The lavatory used by the other residents of Belur Math was a separate building, away from the monks' residential quarters. Bushes and trees surrounded it. In those early days poisonous snakes infested the area. There were no electric lights in the monastery then, so the monks used primitive kerosene lanterns. It was quite risky for them to use the lavatory during the dark hours of the night. But Bagha used to accompany the monks at night, walking ahead of them as though to ensure their safety. Bagha would bark and alert the monks when he sensed the presence of snakes.

Part II

When Swami Vivekananda passed away, his body was cremated on the grounds of Belur Math. During the entire cremation, Bagha remained seated close to the funeral pyre and wouldn't move. Even after it was over, he sat there for a long time, apparently overwhelmed by grief. He couldn't be persuaded even to eat or drink that day.

After Swami Vivekananda passed away, two European devotees, Mother Sevier and Christina, came to Belur Math for a visit. There was no accommodation for women devotees in the monastery, so they pitched a tent on the lawn and camped there for a few days. On his own, Bagha would protect them at night. He wouldn't allow any animals—not even a frog—to come close to the tent.

In course of time Bagha died, and his dead body was consigned to the river. During the outgoing tide, the river carried the body away. But along with the incoming tide, the body returned to Belur Math and stayed on the riverbank. The monks then picked up Bagha's body and buried it under a sandalwood tree in Belur Math.[7]

When Swami Shivananda was President of the Ramakrishna Order, he was given two pet dogs by a devotee. They were pedigree dogs from Sarail, a place in East Bengal renowned for that special breed of dogs. Sarail dogs resemble greyhounds, but are of indigenous origin. It should be mentioned here that following a widely practiced religious tradition, dogs, even pet ones, are not allowed to enter the monastery buildings and the temple, because they are considered unclean. They can take shelter on the veranda, but are not allowed to enter the rooms

---

7. The source of the stories about Bagha is the Bengali book *Pashujatir Manovritti* by Mahendra Nath Dutta.

of the monastery. Even though Kelo and Bhulo were not allowed to enter the buildings, Swami Shivananda made sure that his dogs were regularly given proper food.

Swami Shivananda would sometimes stand upstairs on the balcony outside his room, and throw pieces of bread to his dogs down in the courtyard as a treat. The dogs would jump and catch the bread in mid-air. This made Swami Shivananda very happy. He would sometimes point his finger at the dogs and say, "They're my dogs, and I'm Sri Ramakrishna's dog!"

A brahmachari named Taraprasanna was asked to take care of Kelo and Bhulo. He would take the dogs for a swim in the river Ganga. The river is about one mile wide at that point. The brahmachari and the dogs would swim in the river every day for quite sometime. Every evening, Brahmachari Taraprasanna and the other monks of Belur Math would go and salute Swami Shivananda. Swami Shivananda would invariably ask Taraprasanna, "How far did the dogs swim today?" And Taraprasanna would give a glowing report on the swimming skill of the dogs. It would make Swami Shivananda very happy. After taking his final vows, Taraprasanna became Swami Swayamprabhananda. I lived nearly two years with him in our Shillong ashrama when I was a young brahmachari. The swami was then the head of the ashrama. We heard the above story from him at that time.

It usually takes nine years for a brahmachari to qualify for the final vows of monastic life. Swami Swayamprabhananda told us that he didn't have to wait nine years to become a swami. Swami Shivananda was so pleased with his dedicated service to Kelo and Bhulo that he was permitted to take his final vows one or two years earlier than usual.

Part II

I spent a total of about thirteen years in Belur Math. During that period there were no pet dogs in Belur Math, but there were a fairly large number of stray dogs that had come and taken shelter on the monastery grounds. Previously I hadn't much knowledge about the behavior of dogs. But after watching the dogs of Belur Math, I came to learn quite a bit.

There were about fifteen dogs, all of them mongrels, living on the extensive grounds of the monastery. Most of them were male. I noticed that they had a distinct society of their own. Their chief was one particularly strong male dog.

In the monastery an average of two hundred persons, including servants and guests, would eat every day. As there were no refrigerators in the kitchen, all the leftover food would be given to the dogs. As a result the dogs were pretty well-fed and healthy. At their mealtime, the lead dog would be the first one to eat. They had a well-defined pecking order. Any violation of that order would be corrected by the snarling and occasional biting by the lead dog.

Whenever any strange male dog would enter the Belur Math compound, all the male dogs of the monastery, led by the lead dog, would immediately attack the stranger. But the female dogs would remain quiet. Yet when a strange female dog would enter the monastery grounds, all the female dogs would attack the dog and fight with her. The male dogs would remain quiet and indifferent.

Usually, intruding, stray dogs would hastily leave the compound after being attacked by the Belur Math dogs. Once in a great while, after being attacked, the intruder would immediately lie down on his back in a gesture of submission. Then the monastery dogs would stop barking, and would give up their aggressive behavior. The intruder would then slowly stand up with his tail between his legs, maintaining a safe distance from the pack. At mealtime he would be treated like a pariah by the other dogs. After all the other dogs had eaten, he would get his chance to eat.

As the days would pass, the intruder would gradually straighten his tail and bring it back to its normal height. He would then be seen flattering the lead dog every now and then by licking the lead dog's face or grooming his fur. In this way, the intruder would gradually be accepted as a member of the pack. After that, with great enthusiasm, he would join the other dogs of the pack in chasing out other intruding dogs.

When the lead dog of the monastery became old, two younger dogs that were apparently siblings from the same litter challenged him. They fought and chased the lead dog out of the pack. Then they took the lead dog's position. The deposed lead dog took shelter in the courtyard of our charitable clinic building, which was away from the main grounds of the monastery. One kind-hearted swami would give food to him every day until the dog died of old age.

The two new lead dogs lived in the meadow north of the original monastery building where Swami Vivekananda and some other disciples of Sri Ramakrishna had lived. Swami Vivekananda's room on the second floor of the building is maintained as a shrine, and many of his personal effects are kept there. Next to Swami Vivekananda's room, a veranda with a staircase on each side has been built. Visitors can go up the staircases and view the swami's room through two glass windows. The two lead dogs instinctively guarded that area at night.

Once there was a burglary in Belur Math. The burglars came in the early hours of the morning by boat, and stole some suitcases that were in Swami Vivekananda's room. Hoping that the suitcases contained valuables, they took them out to the bank of the river Ganga and broke them open. There was nothing in them except Swami Vivekananda's clothes. The disappointed burglars scattered the clothes on the riverbank and left. But, before committing the burglary, they fed the lead dogs some food laced with poison. In the morning we found their dead bodies lying in the meadow. Sad though we were at their death, some of us felt that they had had a glorious death, because they had sacrificed their lives trying to protect our beloved Swami Vivekananda's room.

TO DRINK MILK OR TO DO SPIRITUAL PRACTICE?

SWAMI VISHUDDHANANDA
(1883–1962)

"I was fortunate to have lived with a God-realized soul for a number of years," said Swami Videhananda (1906–1984), popularly known as Gangacharan Maharaj.

I was then in my late thirties, and Gangacharan Maharaj must have been in his sixties. I asked him, "Who was that God-realized soul?"

Gangacharan Maharaj replied, "I'm speaking of revered Swami Vishuddhananda. He was that God-realized soul. I stayed with him in our Ranchi Morabadi ashrama for a few years when I was a junior monk. He was then the head of the ashrama."

"How did you know that he was a God-realized soul?" I asked.

Gangacharan Maharaj replied, "We knew about his exemplary spiritual life, and had heard that he had experienced God. But we wanted to know if the information was correct. One evening, during our evening monastic class in the monastery, we asked him, 'Maharaj, Have you experienced God?'

"At first he was extremely reluctant to answer our question. But we wouldn't let him go. We insistently went on requesting him to tell us the truth. Eventually, he yielded to our request. He said that in 1917 he and Swami Madhavananda were performing *tapasya* (spiritual austerities) in Varanasi for a while. At that time, he developed an intense yearning to experience God. He had heard that the saint Tulsidas had had the vision of God on the holy Chitrakut Hill not too far from Varanasi. This thought triggered in his mind a great desire to go and visit Chitrakut.

"Arriving there, he found some accommodation in a local priest's *(panda's)* home. The very first day, while lying awake in his room, he got the vision of God. The experience overwhelmed him with intense spiritual bliss. This condition lasted for three days."

Swami Vishuddhananda was one of the early disciples of the Holy Mother Sri Sarada Devi. Even as a young monk, Swami Brahmananda, one of the foremost saintly disciples of Sri Ramakrishna, acknowledged the exalted spiritual state of his mind. Once, Swami Brahmananda, then President of the Ramakrishna

Order, sent young Swami Vishuddhananda to assist Swami Ramakrishnananda in our Madras ashrama. In introducing Swami Vishuddhananda, Swami Brahmananda wrote to Swami Ramakrishnananda, "I am sending a monk whose mind is always absorbed in God."

In addition to the above, Gangacharan Maharaj told us another very interesting anecdote about Swami Vishuddhananda. One day a Marwari merchant came to him in the Ranchi Morabadi ashrama. The merchant wanted to give a gift of a milk cow to the monks in the ashrama. The financial condition of the ashrama was not good. Swami Vishuddhananda had been suffering from an ulcer in his stomach. His doctor had prescribed milk in his diet. But with the meager income of the ashrama, it was not possible to buy enough milk for him, what to speak of milk for the junior monks. So the proposed gift of a milk cow appeared to be a godsend.

Swami Vishuddhananda called the monks together and said to them, "This kind gentleman wants to give us a milk cow. If we accept the gift it will be an added responsibility for you. You will have to take care of the cow. As a result, there will be less time for your meditation and other spiritual practices. So I ask you to choose between these two things: Do you want to drink milk, or do you want to do your spiritual practice?"

The monks replied, "Maharaj, rather than drinking milk, we would prefer to do our spiritual practices."

Their answer pleased Swami Vishuddhananda. He then told the merchant, "We are sorry. We cannot accept the cow. Instead, may I suggest that you give us some money every month to buy milk for the monks?"

According to Hindu tradition, making a gift of a milk cow

to holy people brings abundant merits. The merchant was not sure if the alternative suggested by Swami Vishuddhananda would produce similar results. Therefore he did not agree, and left the ashrama.

Swami Vishuddhananda eventually became the eighth President of the Ramakrishna Order.

⧗ A TRUE KARMA-YOGI

SWAMI RUDRANANDA
(1901–1985)

It was the home of Chennaiya Gaunder in the town of Nadi in Fiji. Chennaiya had a special guest in his home that night, Swami Rudrananda, the head of the Ramakrishna Mission center in Nadi. It was midnight. Chennaiya had been sleeplessly tossing and turning in his bed for the past three hours, greatly perturbed by a catastrophe that had happened to the Ramakrishna Mission center the day before. Its only residential building had been gutted by fire. In the silence of the night, Chennaiya could hear the regular, peaceful breathing of Swami Rudrananda sleeping in the next room. The swami had had to come and stay in Chennaiya's home, because the fire at the ashrama had made him homeless.

Many years before, the swami had come from India at the invitation of the Indian immigrants in Fiji, and had started a high school in Nadi. The school was for the children of Indian laborers working in the sugarcane plantations owned by the British. The very idea of laborers getting educated alarmed the plantation owners. They feared that the educated children of the laborers would seek other kinds of employment, creating a short supply of laborers in the future. That's why, overtly and covertly, they and their accomplices had for years created problems for the swami. The suspicious fire in the ashrama building appeared to be a case of arson.

While sleeplessly tossing and turning in bed, Chennaiya remembered how hard and lovingly the swami had worked over the years to build the ashrama, and to get the school going. Chennaiya had always been an ardent supporter and admirer of Swami Rudrananda. When the swami's beautiful ashrama was burnt down to the ground, he invited the swami to stay in his home as an honored guest. With great anxiety, Chennaiya wondered how long it would take the swami to rebuild the ashrama.

The whole night he was unable to sleep, because of worries about the swami. Yet, he was amazed that the swami himself slept so peacefully in the next room. It was as though the destruction of the ashrama building, for which the swami had labored so hard and for so many years, did not affect him at all! Chennaiya had read that a karma-yogi is not attached to anything. He performs action without expecting any fruits. Chennaiya now knew, without any doubt, that Swami Rudrananda was a true karma-yogi.

At daybreak, Swami Rudrananda, as was his habit, got up from bed, showered, did his meditation, and came out of his room for breakfast. He looked fresh and well rested. When he saw Chennaiya he said enthusiastically, "Chennaiya, it looks like we have a lot of work ahead of us. We have to start building the ashrama again. I am sure Sri Ramakrishna will help us."

With the financial cooperation of his friends and well-wishers, Swami Rudrananda was able to rebuild the ashrama. The new building was much better than the previous one. It was made of cement concrete and was completely fireproof. The high school run by the ashrama is now considered one of the best in Fiji.

⧗ REMINISCENCES ABOUT SWAMI PRABHANANDA I

SWAMI PRABHANANDA I
(1901–1938)

Swami Prabhananda I, more popularly known as Ketaki Maharaj, lived a life of dedication unparalleled in the history of our Order. I saw him in Shillong when I was five years old. He was staying in the house of our next-door neighbor, Snehalata Dhar, as a guest. Ketaki Maharaj was then completely bedridden, and suffering from a kind of virus-related muscular atrophy. There was no cure for it at that time. Some young men were taking care of his nursing and other physical needs.

Every day many visitors, both men and women, would come to see him. The elders wouldn't allow children to enter his room, thinking that it would disturb the swami. When nobody was around I would sometimes sneak into his room and watch him from a distance. I could smell some medication in his room—perhaps the smell of some ointment that would be massaged over his body. As soon as I would enter the room, he would smile at me. He wouldn't talk to me, or anything. He would just smile. Then I would feel embarrassed and would quickly leave his room.

Eventually, as a young man, I started thinking of leading a life of renunciation. Those thoughts somehow brought Ketaki Maharaj to mind. His memory gave me great strength and inspiration. I remembered his wonderfully winning smile that was unaffected by his incurable illness. I also remembered his death-defying quiet courage that only saintly souls could display.

By that time I had also heard about his wonderful humanitarian work in the Khasi Hills. In 1927 he was sent by the Ramakrishna Mission to work among the tribal people in the Khasi Hills. He was then 27 years old. Working hard for ten years, he established the Ramakrishna ashramas in Shella, Cherrapunji, and Shillong.

Ketaki Maharaj learnt the Khasi language within three months of his arrival in the Khasi Hills. He first started a night school in Shella that was gradually made into a junior high school (M.E. school) for students up to the sixth grade. The swami also started a high school in Cherrapunji, and wrote some text books in the Khasi language. The educational work that he started in Cherrapunji faced the opposition of local Christians, to whom the idea of a Hindu organization starting any school there was not desirable. To counteract their opposition, Ketaki Maharaj quickly formed a committee consisting of the prominent men of Cherrapunji, both Christian and non-Christian, to whom he entrusted the work of organizing the school, himself remaining in the background as far as possible. This wise move proved to be a great success.

The village of Shella is in the foothills of the Khasi Hills, while the town of Cherrapunji is at an altitude of about 3,500 feet. At that time there was no road between Shella and Cherrapunji suitable for vehicles. People had to climb 3,000 feet on foot to reach Cherrapunji. The journey entailed climbing hundreds of steps hewn out of rocks on the steep mountainside. Even the local people found it an extremely strenuous task to climb so many steps. But Ketaki Maharaj frequently did it—sometimes three or four times a week—in order to take care of the school in Cherrapunji. Sometimes he would climb up to Cherrapunji in the morning, and return to Shella the same evening.

While stationed at the Cherrapunji ashrama as a brahmachari for about a year in 1960, I met an elderly Khasi gentleman named Shagen Babu in Shella who had known Ketaki Maharaj. He told me how astounded they were at seeing Ketaki Maharaj accomplish the superhuman feat of climbing back and forth to Cherrapunji so many times a week. While speaking of Ketaki Maharaj's great love for the Khasi people, Shagen Babu broke down in tears.

Ketaki Maharaj blended in well with the people whom he had come to serve. He lived among them, ate with them, shared their joys and sorrows, educated them to be self-sufficient, and taught them the harmony of religions as lived and preached by Sri Ramakrishna. He tried to educate them without any strings attached. His inspiration came from Swami Vivekananda, the founder of the Ramakrishna Mission. Swami Vivekananda had formed the Mission to create a new band of sannyasis (all-renouncing monks), whose motto was to strive for their own spiritual enlightenment, and also to work for the well-being of the world. Once the swami said to some junior monks, "I love you all so much, yet I wish that you die serving others. That will make me happy."

Ketaki Maharaj had always been an idealistic young man. In his late teens, as an undergraduate student, he was active in India's Non-co-operation Movement of 1920-21. Like many other young men in India, he was determined to sacrifice his life to free his country from British rule.

With another young man, he rented a small house in the city of Dacca to hold "secret party meetings to plan and direct subversive activities against the British." In order to hide their real intention from the police and the public, one of them spent long hours loudly practicing vocal music. In those days, Mahatma Gandhi had introduced a movement based on his political philosophy of non-violence. The symbol of that movement was the hand-operated spinning wheel. Thousands of followers of Mahatma Gandhi started using these noisy spinning wheels to produce yarn. The yarn would be used by handlooms to weave coarse cloth for the Indians.

The two young men procured spinning wheels, and operated them noisily at all odd hours of the day and night to let the neighbors and the police know that they were believers in Gandhian non-violence! But obviously they overdid their singing and spinning routine. Eventually many of the neighbors objected to their loud singing and the harsh squeaking of their spinning wheels.

Some of the neighbors "began to throw rocks at the house whenever the singing started at an inconvenient hour." An Anglo-Indian neighbor got so angry that one day he rushed into the house of the two young men and threatened to shoot them with his pistol unless they stopped the noise generated by their spinning wheels. Ketaki Maharaj "sprang to his feet and baring his chest said, 'Shoot me if you dare, but I am not going to stop spinning.'

"The Anglo-Indian gentleman realized that he had before him two desperate men who would stop at nothing if they were provoked further. Cursing them, he quietly withdrew. Ketaki felt that it was time that they left the place, for the Anglo-Indian gentleman was sure to report them to the police who, already on their trail in connection with their political activities elsewhere, would soon appear and take them in custody under some pretext or other. For some time after this, they began to drift, having no fixed aim and no fixed address, for the police were constantly after them."[8]

It was during this period that they began to visit the local branch of the Ramakrishna Mission, because of their great regard for Swami Vivekananda and his guru, Sri Ramakrishna. As a result of these visits, they gradually gained the conviction that service to the whole of mankind was even better than patriotism. The ideal of the Ramakrishna Mission to serve God in man irrespective of nationality, religion, color, or caste appealed to them greatly. Ketaki, the older of the two, decided to join the Ramakrishna Order as a monk. He joined the Dacca branch of the Order. As monks are addressed in the Ramakrishna Order as *Maharaj,* Ketaki came to be known as Ketaki Maharaj. After taking the final vows of monastic life he became Swami Prabhananda I.

Around that time, news reached the Dacca ashrama that

8. The quoted portions are from an article by Swami Lokeswarananda.

some Khasis were anxious to have some organization come and start schools in their hills. They wanted to make sure that they could safely send their children to school without exposing them to the danger of sectarian religious propaganda. Ketaki Maharaj was asked by the Dacca ashrama to go and explore the possibilities of starting such schools for the Khasis. That is how he came to the Khasi Hills.

The extreme physical strain he went through day after day gradually affected his health. Finally he became a total invalid. But during the short period of ten years that he was able to work, he accomplished a lot. He started a junior high school (M.E. school) in Shella, a high school in Cherrapunji, and an ashrama in Shillong. Shillong was then the capital of the province of Assam.

His physical condition was deteriorating quickly, and he didn't want to be a burden on the Order. He requested the managing committee that managed the three ashramas to relieve him of all his responsibilities, and to carry on the work without him. "They agreed to do their best, but begged that he continue to guide them so long as that was possible. From the time Ketaki Maharaj ceased to be actively involved in the work, he refused to allow the committee to spend any money on him."

Snehalata Dhar, a devotee of Sri Ramakrishna, offered to spare two rooms of her house in Shillong for use by the swami. Ketaki Maharaj accepted the offer and moved to her house. A friend (Dr. Manoranjan Goswami) supplied his food daily. But he stayed in that house just for a few months.

"Meanwhile, his relations at home (a village in the county of Sylhet in Bengal), and especially the young people of his village who had heard about his colorful life, were pressing him to come back to the village to spend his last days there. Seeing that he was too much of a burden on the people who were looking after him in Shillong, he returned to his village after more than a decade. The whole village began to look upon him as if he was their most prized possession. Although life was fast ebbing away and he knew that the end might come any day, he did not rest but kept himself busy encouraging the young men of the village to spend their free time in the service of the community. It was at his instance that an organization soon came into being through which the young men of the village began to care for the weaker sections of the village population. It was at that time that the village people woke up one day to see a crowd of strange people winding their way to Ketaki Maharaj's house. It was the Khasis who had come to pay their last homage to their benefactor. No eye was dry when they arrived at his house or when, some days later, they took leave of him. It was as if he was waiting for this last meeting with the people he had come to regard as his own, for Ketaki Maharaj, not long after this, quietly slipped into death on a cold morning in 1938. He was barely thirty-seven then!"

SOME REMINISCENCES ABOUT SWAMI BHUTESHANANDA

The earliest memories that I have of Swami Bhuteshananda are of a shaven-headed, dark-complexioned monk in his mid-thirties. He wore the usual ochre robe of a sannyasi, and used a pair of canvas shoes of the same color. I would sometimes see him riding a bicycle up and down the hilly roads of Shillong. Normally he looked serious and somewhat grave, but he had a beautiful, winning smile. Even though he was young, he was highly respected by the Ramakrishna devotees of Shillong.

SWAMI BHUTESHANANDA
(1901–1998)

The devotees knew him by the name Bijoy Maharaj.

One morning, when I was about seven years old, I went to the homoeopathic pharmacy of Dr. Manoranjan Goswami. Dr. Goswami was a close relative of ours, and his pharmacy was just a few steps away from our home. We were very fond of him. I would often go to his pharmacy just to see him. That morning, while sitting in his pharmacy, I saw Swami Bhuteshananda arrive on his bike. He got off the bike and entered the pharmacy. Saluting the swami Dr. Goswami asked, "Bijoy Maharaj, what's the news? What brings you here this morning?"

Swami Bhuteshananda replied, "An invitation!"

Dr. Goswami was quite surprised. He was a good friend and supporter of the ashrama. He knew that the celebrations at the ashrama when devotees are invited were already over. Besides, such invitations usually came through letters. The swamis didn't personally come and invite devotees. So he said, "Is the invitation for any new celebration in the ashrama? I thought that the usual celebrations for this year are already over."

Swami Bhuteshananda smiled and said, "No, I'm not talking about that kind of invitation; I've come to invite myself to your home for dinner!"

Dr. Goswami immediately folded his hands in salutation,

and joyfully said to Swami Bhuteshananda, "I shall consider it a great honor to have you come and bless my humble home any time you want. When can I invite you to have dinner with us?"

Swami Bhuteshananda replied, "One of my brother monks has come to the ashrama for a visit. I don't know whether you know or not, but our ashrama food is awfully poor. So far as I am concerned, I'm quite satisfied with it, but I thought it would be nice if at least once we could provide our guest with a better meal. Will it be all right if we come tomorrow?"

Dr. Goswami said that it would be fine with him. Swami Bhuteshananda and the guest swami came next day and had dinner in Dr. Goswami's home. The doctor had made arrangements for a sumptuous dinner.

Swami Bhuteshananda was the head of the Shillong ashrama from 1936 to 1945. During that period, through his efforts the finances of the ashrama became somewhat better, although the standard of food for the resident monks remained just about the same. A small but beautiful temple was built; a small home for indigent students was started; and the number of devotees became much larger. I remember him giving discourses on the *Srimad Bhagavatam* and other scriptures. He was transferred in 1945 from the Shillong ashrama to the Rajkot ashrama as its head. He worked there for twenty-one years, until he was brought to our headquarters in Belur Math in 1966 to be an assistant secretary. I was then one of the junior monks working at the headquarters office. I was happy to meet him there after all those years.

We all knew Swami Bhuteshananda was a disciple of Swami Saradananda, a saintly disciple of Sri Ramakrishna. Swami

Saradananda was renowned for his extraordinarily calm and serene nature. Nothing could perturb or agitate him. Once Swami Vivekananda praised him saying, "He is as cold-blooded as a sand fish; he never becomes angry." It seems Swami Bhuteshananda inherited that wonderful quality from his guru.

One year our Order was conducting drought relief operations in the state of Bihar. Swami Bhuteshananda got the report that a junior monastic supervisor of one of the relief operations hadn't been following the instructions from the headquarters properly, so he asked the supervisor to come and see him. The supervisor, though efficient, had a problem with his ego. When he came to see Swami Bhuteshananda, he lost his temper and started shouting insults at the swami. We were all astounded at the supervisor's behavior. But Swami Bhuteshananda remained perfectly calm, serene, and unperturbed. Such behavior by a junior monastic warranted disciplinary action, but Swami Bhuteshananda quietly ignored the incident. As was his nature, he went on treating the monk with the same brotherly love and affection as before. Returning to Bihar, the monk ran the relief operations following the instructions of the headquarters, but two or three years later he left the Order of his own accord.

I visited India from Seattle a few times after Swami Bhuteshananda had become our President. During one of those visits he said to me, "You want to know what my attitude is? I want to bring everyone in. I don't want to leave anyone out." He wanted to bring everyone within the perimeter of his selfless motherly love.

I have already mentioned that Swami Bhuteshananda had known me since I was a young boy in Shillong. During one of my visits to India, while in my early sixties, I went to see him in Belur Math. When I bowed down and saluted him, he stroked my head full of graying hair with great affection and said with a smile to the other monks present, "Look at him! I've known him since he was a boy wearing half pants. And now his hair has turned gray!"

One day a monk said to him, "We expect you to live for at least 100 years."

Swami Bhuteshananda immediately replied, "Believe me, I don't at all keep track of my age." He was then 94 years old. Why should he? Where is the time for keeping track of such petty matters when one has engaged one's heart and soul in the service of God!

Swami Bhuteshananda had great command over the Sanskrit language. Swami Gambhirananda, who preceded Swami Bhuteshananda as President of our Order, was renowned for his great scholarship. He authored many books, and translated many difficult Sanskrit scriptural texts, such as the *Upanishads*, into Bengali and English. More than once I saw him consult Swami Bhuteshananda on the meaning of some extremely difficult Sanskrit texts he had been translating. Swami Bhuteshananda also knew English, Bengali, and Gujarati very well.

Even though a great scholar, such was his humility that at his own initiative he never wrote a single book. But over the years he gave many deep and spiritually uplifting scriptural discourses, both in Bengali and English. Many of those discourses were recorded by others and later published as books. Despite his erudition Swami Bhuteshananda belonged to that select group of scholars who are completely devoid of scholastic vanity.

The kind of hierarchy that exists in some monastic organizations isn't there in the Ramakrishna Order. The spiritual qualities that a monk possesses alone make him worthy of respect. A higher administrative position in our Order does not necessarily mean a position of enhanced respectability. A higher position only means greater responsibility to be humbly carried out in the right spirit of service. I have closely known at least three Presidents of our Order. All were completely devoid of a false ego. Their high position didn't affect them at all. Swami Bhuteshananda was one of them.

We have radioactivity detectors to detect the presence of radioactivity. But there are no *saint detectors* available in the market to judge or detect saintliness. Many use miraculous powers as the only criterion to judge a saint. "Can he levitate?" they ask. "Can he cure illnesses? Can he tell the future? Can he pass through solid walls? Can he materialize objects out of thin air?"

Once while I was visiting Brazil, someone asked me, "What do you think of materializing things out of thin air?"

I replied, "I think those who materialize things don't have the money to buy them."

I am glad that I, and other monks of the Ramakrishna Order, don't belong to that crowd of mystery-mongers. A saint has to be judged by the qualities of unselfishness, truthfulness, and honesty. He has to be physically and mentally pure. He mustn't crave name, fame, power, or position. His heart and intellect should be equally well-developed. He must be loving, compassionate, cheerful, intelligent, and in full control of himself. In addition, he must possess a good sense of humor.

Judging by the above criteria, I'm sure that Swami Bhuteshananda was a saintly soul. Yet, if he were alive, this assessment of his spirituality would cause him great embarrassment. The humility of a genuine saint doesn't allow him to be aware of his saintliness.

In his nineties Swami Bhuteshananda underwent successful open-heart surgery. After the operation his doctors advised him to take some mild exercise in the morning. Following the doctors' instructions, he walked every morning for fifteen or twenty minutes along the closed corridor of his residential quarters. Two monastic attendants accompanied him during his walk. One day during his morning walk, he said to us with a smile, "People say I've become the President of the Ramakrishna Order. But I feel that I am the same monk who was in the Shillong ashrama sixty years ago. The only difference is that now I have a bunch of sevaks (attendants) around me!" His indifference to position revealed his genuine humility, a quality present only among saintly souls.

Another hallmark of his personality was his keen sense of humor. During his presidency, the monks would visit him every day after breakfast for nearly half an hour. That period was as spiritually inspiring as it was entertaining. After saluting him,

MONKS ENJOYING THE HUMOR OF
SWAMI BHUTESHANANDA

the monks would ask him questions connected with spiritual life, sometimes in a very witty and humorous fashion. Swami Bhuteshananda's answers—always at least as witty and humorous as the questions—would elicit loud and frequent laughter. He had an exemplary sense of humor, the kind of humor that never hurts or ridicules anyone. It only gives pure joy to the listeners.

Sri Chaitanya Mahaprabhu, a divine incarnation, used to say that a genuine lover of God has two characteristics. He does not crave honor or respect for himself, but is always eager to respect and honor others. These two characteristics were prominent in Swami Bhuteshananda.

In 1974 our Order posted me to Seattle. On my way to the United States, I stopped in Japan at the Vedanta Society in Zushi City and attended the dedication ceremony of the society's first building. That visit gave me an opportunity to meet the prominent members of the society. Two years later they sent me an invitation to visit the society for a month in the summer, which I accepted. After that visit, they requested me to visit them every summer. Thus, I visited the Vedanta society of Zushi for six consecutive years, staying there for four or five weeks each time.

During that period, the members became quite eager to have a larger building for the society to use as the ashrama. Mr. V. S. Noma, then secretary of the society, and others enthusiastically solicited funds, and within a short time this dream became a reality. The construction of the second building was mainly due to the generosity of the late Mr. H. R. Gajria, an Indian industrialist whom I had come to know in Japan. At my request, he donated the yen equivalent of us $150,000.00 to the building fund. The late Mrs. Haru Nakai also gave a very large donation.

Later Swami Bhuteshananda started visiting the society from India, blessing many Japanese devotees with spiritual initiation. Eventually Swami Siddharthananda came as the first resident swami for the Zushi Vedanta society.

Swami Bhuteshananda never forgot what little part I had played in the early growth of the Zushi Vedanta society. During my visits to India, when I would go and see him in Belur Math, on at least three occasions he told the monks present there, "The Japan Vedanta center is ours today mainly due to the efforts of Bhaskarananda."

The purpose of writing this apparently superfluous autobiographical episode is not to glorify myself, but to point out how Swami Bhuteshananda, who was the least interested in praise, honor or appreciation for himself, was always eager to praise others, even a very insignificant junior brother monk like me!

Great souls like Swami Bhuteshananda are like so many fragrant incense sticks. As they burn, their spiritual fragrance permeates the atmosphere. Even when burnt to ashes, their fragrance lingers on. Swami Bhuteshananda has shed his mortal coil, but the spiritual fragrance of his holy life will continue inspiring people for a long time to come, making their lives holier and more spiritually meaningful.

SWAMI PRANAVATMANANDA— AN UNFORGETTABLE MONK

The confluence of the holy river Ganga and the Bay of Bengal is called *Gangasagar*. It is a very holy place in India. Once a year, on an auspicious day in winter, a great fair is held there. The local people call this fair *Gangasagar Mela*. Thousands of pilgrims from all over India come to the Gangasagar Mela to take a dip in the confluence of the Ganga and the sea. They come with the deep faith in their hearts that such a bath will free them from their sins, and bring them liberation from the cycle of repeated births and deaths.

Along with the pilgrims and holy men and women, many

Part II

SWAMI PRANAVATMANANDA
(1904–1975)

traders come to sell a great variety of goods. And along with them, quite a few crooks and charlatans come to swindle unsuspecting and gullible pilgrims.

In Hindu tradition donating milk cows to brahmins is considered a meritorious act. Several years ago a swindler came to the fair grounds. He wore the sacred thread of a brahmin. He brought along with him an assistant and a milk cow.

The assistant loudly announced to all the passers-by, "Friends, don't lose this opportunity to earn merits and go to heaven. Please buy this cow and donate her to this venerable brahmin. The price of the cow is only five rupees." Usually the price of a good milk cow at that time was at least two hundred rupees. Some gullible pilgrim would pay five rupees for the cow, and then donate her to the brahmin. The same cow would again be sold to another pilgrim, who would also give her to the brahmin as a gift. In this manner the crooks enjoyed a brisk business.

A swami observed this from a distance and wanted to teach the crooks a lesson. He asked one of his companions to buy the cow. Then the swami walked quickly away, pulling the cow behind him. The crooks were alarmed by this turn of events. The assistant ran after the swami and shouted, "Sir, why are you going away with the cow? Won't you donate her to the brahmin? Don't you want to earn merits and go to heaven?"

The swami replied with a smile, "No, I'm not in a rush to earn merit or go to heaven! I've no intention of donating the cow to anybody. I just need this cow."

Meanwhile, the brahmin ran up to the swami and pleaded desperately, "Sir, please forgive me. I'm really a brahmin, although my behavior is not appropriate for a brahmin. I'm very poor and this is my only means of livelihood. I live in a nearby village. During the fair I earn a little money from the pilgrims in this devious manner. That's how I maintain my family. Please don't take away this cow. This is the only cow that I have."

The swami felt compassion for the poor brahmin and returned the cow. The swami was a monk of the Ramakrishna Order. His name was Swami Pranavatmananda, popularly known in the Order as Pashupati Maharaj.

CHARLES MATHIAS

As is obvious from the above story, the swami was very witty and humorous. He was also endowed with great compassion, purity of heart, and devotion to God. One of his special characteristics was that he was always cheerful. He was also an excellent storyteller. His stories, usually with spiritual content, were so humorous that his listeners laughed and laughed until their bellies ached.

He often talked about his pilgrimage to the Himalayas and about other places that he had visited. For many years he traveled from village to village giving audiovisual presentations on the life and teachings of Sri Ramakrishna. He very much wanted the village folks to know about Sri Ramakrishna and to benefit from his teachings.

He knew how to model with clay very well. Every year he would make beautiful clay images of Divine Mother Durga for the annual worship of the deity in the Shillong ashrama. Following an age-old tradition, the image would be immersed in a local river after the worship. That's why it was necessary to construct a new image every year. And Swami Pranavatmananda, as long as he was physically able, would come to the Shillong ashrama every year, and lovingly make the image of the Divine Mother Durga.

The swami would come to the Shillong ashrama nearly two months before the worship, and would start modeling the image with the help of an assistant, nicknamed "Shani Thakur." After the image was painted, it would be draped in a beautiful sari and adorned with decorations. I, along with other brahmacharis of the Shillong ashrama, sometimes helped in decorating the image under the swami's guidance.

Swami Pranavatmananda was also an adept in ritualistic

worship. He trained some brahmacharis to perform the elaborate ritualistic worship of the Divine Mother Durga. The worship would be held on five consecutive days. He was always present during the worship as *tantradharaka* (guide and prompter), and would guide the brahmachari performing the worship.

Our scriptures say that when the worshipper chants the sacred mantras of invocation, the deity becomes manifest in the image. During every worship of the Divine Mother Durga, Swami Pranavatmananda would want to be sure that the deity had manifested in the image.

The image of Mother Durga has ten arms. In course of the worship, the brahmachari had to put a flower smeared with fragrant sandal paste on one of the ten hands of the deity. Swami Pranavatmananda would silently say to himself, "I'll take it as a sure sign that Mother Durga has become manifested in the image if the brahmachari puts the flower on that particular hand of the Mother." And invariably the brahmachari would put the flower on the hand chosen by the swami. Thus he would be 100% convinced that Mother Durga had come and was accepting the worship offered to Her.

On the last day of the worship, following the ritualistic tradition, the worshipper bids farewell to the Mother, and requests Her to come again from Her celestial abode the following year to accept his worship. During the farewell, Swami Pranavatmananda, overwhelmed by intense spiritual emotion, would shed tears. Like a child, he didn't want the Divine Mother to go away, leaving him behind.

The authorities of the Order asked him several times to take charge of one or the other of its branch centers. At one time, he was made the head of the Contai center. But after a few years he asked to be relieved of that responsibility, as he felt that the message of Sri Ramakrishna should be spread among the masses. So with the blessings of Swami Madhavananda, then General Secretary of the Order, he started giving audio-visual presentations on the life and teachings of Sri Rama-krishna in the rural areas in Bengal. Later he learned Hindi, so that he could work in the Hindi-speaking areas as well. He did that work for many years until he became old and began suffering from occasional attacks of gout. Then the authorities placed him in charge of the Gauhati (now renamed Guahati) ashrama.

Once when he was in Gauhati, an interesting incident happened. A gentleman came to the ashrama and wanted to talk to Swami Pranavatmananda privately. At that time the swami was suffering from a severe attack of gout that had made him completely bedridden. The gentleman was told that it wouldn't be possible for him to see the swami. But the gentleman was desperate, and insisted on talking to Swami Pranavatmananda. At last the monks yielded to his request, and with Swami Pranavatmananda's permission, the gentleman was allowed to go and talk to the swami in his bedroom.

After saluting the swami the gentleman said, "Maharaj, I've a grave family problem. That's why I needed to talk to you privately. My only daughter seems to be possessed by a departed spirit. Although I heard about such things, I never believed that a spirit could really possess anyone. But now I've no way of disbelieving it, because it has happened to my own daughter.

"Ever since the possession she has become a completely

different person. The other day the spirit that possesses her asked my wife to give her a bath, and demanded that before her bath, a fragrant hair oil called Javakusum Oil be applied to her hair. When that was done, the spirit said to my wife, 'In the other world we have desires, but we can't satisfy them. It feels so good to have a body again, because I can now fulfill my desires.'

"The spirit demands to be given certain special dishes to eat every day, and unless we meet those demands, it becomes very upset and angry. The spirit also has an uncanny sense of time. If it says, 'Give me food at 1 p.m.' and we bring the food half an hour earlier, it says, 'Why have you brought the food now? It's only 12:30 now. Take back the food; I won't eat until 1 o'clock.' Even though there's no clock in the room, the spirit can sense the correct time.

"But the main reason why I've come to see you, Maharaj, is that the spirit again and again demands, 'Take me to Belur Math!' The spirit seems to have some fondness for Belur Math (the headquarters of the Ramakrishna Order), and we thought that it may listen to you, a monk of the Ramakrishna Order, and agree to leave my daughter's body."

Swami Pranavatmananda felt great compassion for the gentleman. Despite his terribly aching legs that had temporarily made him almost a cripple, he agreed to visit the gentleman's home. The swami was lifted from his bed by an able-bodied monk, and put in a vehicle. When he arrived at the gentleman's home, the swami was helped by that gentleman to go to the haunted girl's room and sit there. As soon as the girl saw the swami, she said to him, "Please take me to Belur Math. I want to live there."

Swami Pranavatmananda said, "Only monks live in Belur Math. You're a girl. You can't live there!"

The girl, speaking like a young child, said, "If they don't allow me to live there, I'll jump into the river. (How the spirit knew that Belur Math was on the bank of the river Ganga is hard to explain!) Then the monks will pull me out of water and let me stay in the monastery."

Swami Pranavatmananda said, "I'm sorry. I don't think it'll work. The monastery is only for monks, no girl can stay there." Then he added, "Why don't you leave this girl? I give you my word; I'll pray to Sri Ramakrishna for your liberation."

At this the spirit said that it would leave the girl a few days later, on a certain day. The swami then returned to the ashrama. He later heard from that gentleman that the spirit truly left his daughter as promised, on that particular day. And his daughter had no memory whatsoever of what had happened to her when the spirit possessed her.

I heard the above story from Swami Pranavatmananda himself.

After I was sent to the United States by our Order to work in the Seattle ashrama, Swami Pranavatmananda wrote me a few letters. In the last letter that I received from him, he wrote in his usual humorous way, "Now I've discovered my escape route from this world. I went to see my doctor the other day for a check-up, and he said that half of my heart is gone!" A few months later I got the news that he had had a sudden heart attack, and had passed away. Knowing him, I could not help thinking that he must have left this world with a smile on his face.

NAREN MAHARAJ AS I REMEMBER HIM

Once, in Belur Math, Naren Maharaj, otherwise known as "Totla (stammerer) Naren Maharaj," was busy conversing with a brother monk. Both were in their seventies at that time. During their conversation the other monk teasingly said to Naren Maharaj, "You're a fool!"

Naren Maharaj smiled and immediately retorted, "What! You're saying that I'm beauti*ful*? Don't you have any eyes? Look at me! I've lost all my teeth. My skin is wrinkled. I now look more like a monkey! How can I be beauti*ful?*" Then both of them burst into hearty laughter.

Naren Maharaj had the wonderful ability to joke at his own expense. He was also very good-hearted. Many years earlier, as a young monk, I worked at the headquarters office in Belur Math for a number of years. Then for a while, I stayed in a building with a few retired, elderly monks. Naren Maharaj was one of them. I was one of the youngest residents in that building. The elderly swamis were naturally affectionate to me.

They all lived a very regular life. They would get up very early in the morning, shower, and then meditate until breakfast time. After breakfast they would go and pay their respects at the four temples in Belur Math, and then would walk around a little inside the large monastery compound. That would be their morning exercise.

I would go to the headquarters office after breakfast, and work there with the other monks. Swami Swananda worked in the correspondence section of our office. He acted something like a private secretary to the General Secretary and the two assistant secretaries of the Order. There was no official designation for his position, but we, the junior monks in the office, humorously referred to him as our *office superintendent.*

On their way back to their residence after their morning walk, Naren Maharaj and some other senior swamis would regularly stop at our department in the headquarters office just to say hello to me. Swami Swananda would humorously refer to them as my "guardian angels."

I respected my guardian angels, but at the same time enjoyed playing innocent jokes on them, which they apparently liked. For example, one day I said to Naren Maharaj, "Sri Ramakrishna said that if a person practices truthfulness for twelve years, whatever words come out of his mouth come true. You have been in the Order for more than fifty years. As you have practiced truthfulness as a monk for so many years, whatever you say must come true. Please bless me, saying, 'May you have nirvikalpa samadhi this very moment.' Then all my spiritual problems will be solved in an instant."

But Naren Maharaj responded, "Thakur (Sri Ramakrishna) will bless you. Who am I to bless?" Nevertheless, the smile that appeared on his face clearly indicated that he had appreciated my joke.

Even though he was advanced in age, Naren Maharaj's health was quite good. For many years he didn't suffer from any illness. But eventually he developed a persistent throat ache needing medical attention. He went to our hospital in Calcutta for a check-up, and the cause of the sore throat was determined to be cancer. Thinking that the news might upset him, the doctors did not tell Naren Maharaj the diagnosis. We at the headquarters office, however, were informed. A few days after his check-up, Naren Maharaj came to see me in our office and asked, "What's the diagnosis? The doctors don't want to tell me anything. Is it something bad?"

I replied, "The doctors hesitated to tell you their diagnosis, thinking that it might upset you. But you are a monk; I see no reason why they should have kept it a secret from you. I can tell you what we've heard from the hospital. They informed us that you've got cancer."

Naren Maharaj was not the least bit affected by the news. He said cheerfully, "Good! Thakur (Sri Ramakrishna) also suffered from the same disease. After all, the body has to perish one way or the other, isn't it?" Then he asked, "How long am I expected to live? Have the doctors given a time limit?"

Now I don't remember exactly what time limit the doctors gave, but I'm sure it was less than a year, and I told him so. Then Naren Maharaj thanked me and left the office with a cheerful face.

Shortly after this I was sent away by the headquarters to work in America. Before my departure, the monks of the headquarters office gave me an informal farewell. And Naren Maharaj, who happened to visit our office just then, was "made" the guest of honor! He joked a lot, and expressly prayed for my future well-being.

When I visited Belur Math two years later, I heard the interesting story of Naren Maharaj's death. After I left India, he was admitted to our hospital in Calcutta and given treatment for his cancer which prolonged his life by a few more months. He was in a special ward meant only for monks. Cheerful as ever, he would greet the other monks every day, saying in English, "Good morning." (Although his mother tongue was Bengali, and the other monks he greeted were not English-speaking, he enjoyed greeting them in English, just for the sake of innocent fun.)

Naren Maharaj knew English quite well. He had studied English literature in his Master's program in the university, but I'm not sure if he ever finished the course. He thought it very funny to greet monks saying "Good morning" in the afternoon, as well as in the evening. Even on the last day of his life, he greeted his fellow patients the same way, and then lay down in bed and peacefully breathed his last.

🕱 DWARAKA MAHARAJ AND HIS STORY OF SHABARI

The great epic *Ramayana* tells us the story of the female ascetic Shabari, whose ashrama was in a forest. As a young girl she had devotedly served some venerable sages in that same forest. Being pleased with her service, they blessed her, saying, "Some day Lord Rama (a divine incarnation) will come with his brother Lakshmana and bless your ashrama. When they come, receive them as your most honored guests. By Lord Rama's grace you will attain the highest heaven."

From that time on, Shabari waited for the visit of Lord Rama with all her heart and soul. Every morning, with great anticipation, she picked the sweetest fruits and berries from the forest for Lord Rama, because the sages hadn't said on which day Lord Rama would come. Every time she heard the soft noise of dry leaves dropping from the trees of the forest, she took that to be the sound of Lord Rama's footsteps and came rushing out of her cottage, looking in vain for Lord Rama.

Gradually the days, months, and finally the years passed, and Shabari still patiently waited to hear the footsteps of Lord Rama. At last, many years later, when Shabari was very old,

Lord Rama finally came to her ashrama. He was extremely pleased with Shabari's single-minded devotion. With his blessings and permission, Shabari lit a sacred fire, entered into it, and gave up her old and decrepit body. By Lord Rama's grace, she then acquired an effulgent heavenly body and ascended to the highest heaven. Thus ends the story of Shabari in the *Ramayana*.

Swami Shiveshananda (1894–1975), also known as Dwaraka Maharaj, had spent most of his monastic life in Belur Math. When I saw him, nearly forty years ago, he was in his late sixties. He was then quite healthy and strong. The younger monks and devotees liked him very much for his loving nature. Many young men, particularly the students of our residential degree college near Belur Math, gave him the nickname *Galpa Maharaj,* meaning the *storyteller swami*. He was really an excellent storyteller. He would usually tell stories from the Hindu mythological literature. And one of his favorite stories, one that he was never tired of telling again and again, was a unique version of the story of Shabari.

"Now I'll tell you a new story of Shabari," he would say, "But do you know who this Shabari was? It was I! Yes, indeed, I was like Shabari when I joined Belur Math as a brahmachari! By that time, I had been initiated by my guru, Mahapurush Maharaj, (Swami Shivananda, President of the Ramakrishna Order at that time) and he lived upstairs in the monastery building.

"The manager swami of the monastery told me, 'Look at the mango and jack-fruit trees in the front yard of the monastery. The yard is constantly littered with dry leaves dropping from them. It will be your duty to keep the yard free of dry leaves. When Mahapurush Maharaj comes out of the monastery building, he mustn't see a courtyard littered with dry leaves.'

"I was happy to get that assignment, and tried to keep the yard meticulously clean. As soon as I would hear the sound of a single leaf dropping to the ground, I would immediately run and pick it up. I would spend the entire day picking up leaves, because I was not sure when my guru would come out into the yard. Thus I became like Shabari. With all the eagerness of my heart, I would wait to hear my guru's footsteps in the yard that I had been trying to keep so meticulously clean."

After saying this much, Dwaraka Maharaj would look at the listeners, pause for a moment, and then say, "You know one thing? While I was busy keeping the yard clean, I didn't know that along with that I had also been unknowingly cleaning something else. And that was my *mind*. Our scriptures say that through dedicated service to God, a person acquires a pure mind. This mind enables the devotee to eventually experience God. Our scriptures also say that the guru and God are one and the same. So you see, picking up leaves from the yard actually became my spiritual practice."

This is how Dwaraka Maharaj would end his wonderful story of Shabari.

SWAMI SANKARANANDA AND TWO SMART ALECKS FROM CALCUTTA

The scriptures tell us about *tanmatras*. These are extremely subtle, invisible particles that are emitted by the bodies of people. Tanmatras can be compared to the subtle fragrance of flowers. The invisible mist of its fragrance surrounds a flower. When you bring your nose inside that mist, you get the fragrance.

SWAMI SANKARANANDA
(1880–1961)

A person, like a fragrant flower, is surrounded by a mist of his or her tanmatras. The tanmatras carry the qualities and characteristics of a person. The tanmatras emitted by a saintly person represent saintly qualities, while the tanmatras of a criminal carry criminal propensities. This is why the Hindu scriptures speak of the importance of keeping holy company. When a person comes inside the mist of the holy tanmatras of a saintly person, those tanmatras can awe a person or even raise that person's mind to a higher spiritual level.

Swami Sankarananda was then the President of the Ramakrishna Order. He was very fair, tall, and broad-shouldered, with large eyes that shone with an inner spiritual light. Even in his late seventies, such was his awe-inspiring spiritual presence that very few would dare speak to him first. They would wait until Swami Sankarananda himself would start the conversation.

Every day during the early hours of the evening, for an hour or so, devotees and monks would be allowed to go to his room and salute him. One day, when the time for salutations was over and the door of Swami Sankarananda's room was closed, two young men arrived from Calcutta. They wanted to see

Swami Sankarananda. They were very politely informed that the interview hour was over, and they wouldn't be able to see the swami. But the young men were two smart alecks from Calcutta. They couldn't be persuaded to leave. They shouted and created quite a commotion. They said that they had a lot to complain about the Ramakrishna Order to its President, and demanded that they be allowed to see Swami Sankarananda immediately.

Eventually the swami's sevak led the young men into Swami Sankarananda's room. As soon as they entered, they obviously became overwhelmed by the spiritual presence (the holy tanmatras) of Swami Sankarananda. For a minute or so they stood there stupefied and completely speechless. Without saying a word, they bowed down, saluted the swami, and quietly left the room.

SWAMI NIRVEDANANDA—A TEACHER TURNED MONK

SWAMI NIRVEDANANDA
(1893–1958)

Before becoming a swami of the Ramakrishna Order, Swami Nirvedananda was known as Suren. Even when quite young, he set himself his life's goal. He decided to remain unmarried and spend his entire life doing philanthropic work. After his university education, he started a small students' home for young men in Calcutta. The students got free food and lodging at the home, and attended different educational institutions in that area. Swami Nirvedananda was the superintendent in charge of the home. He also gave the students additional tutoring whenever needed. Thus he came to be known as Suren Master, meaning "Suren the teacher."

Once the students, with the permission of Suren Master, went to the Dakshineswar Temple for a visit. Suren Master asked them not to visit Belur Math at that time. He didn't want the students to go and disturb the monks. But the students disobeyed him and went there anyway. There they met Brahmachari Jnan Maharaj, who was a disciple of Swami Vivekananda. Jnan Maharaj was easily approachable, and everybody, whether young or old, would feel at ease in his presence. The students had a long conversation with him. During the conversation Jnan Maharaj said to the young men, "Please ask your teacher to come here for a visit."

Even though the students had disobeyed Suren Master, they were not dishonest. They went back to the home and informed their superintendent that they had disobeyed him and gone to see Belur Math. They also told him that Jnan Maharaj had invited him to go there for a visit. After hearing the entire story, Suren Master thought, "As Brahmachari Jnan Maharaj has asked me to see him, let me go and visit Belur Math."

But in this connection, I should mention another incident that has great relevance to this story. For some time past, Suren Master had been suffering from an internal conflict that he couldn't resolve. The conflict was about his life's ideal. Some deeper questions about spiritual life had been perturbing his mind, and he was unable to find the answers. Out of desperation, he decided to do something unconventional. There was a framed picture of Sri Krishna hanging in his room. He wrote

SWAMI PREMANANDA
(1861–1918)

down all his questions on a sheet of paper, folded it, and put it at the bottom of the picture, hoping that it might help him to find the answers.

Several days after the students' visit to Belur Math, Suren Master went there to see Jnan Maharaj. But as soon as he entered the monastery compound, he met Swami Premananda, the manager of Belur Math. Swami Premananda received Suren with much cordiality and love. Then they both sat down in the monastery and started talking. During their conversation Swami Premananda, on his own and without being asked by Suren, raised each and every question that Suren had written down on the sheet of paper in his room. Then following the same order in which the questions had been written, he answered all of them, one by one. Suren was completely astounded. From then onward Suren frequently visited Belur Math.

Eventually he met Swami Shivananda and felt quite drawn to him. One day, when Suren was with Swami Shivananda, Swami Brahmananda, the President of the Ramakrishna Order, entered the room. He glanced at Suren and said to Swami Shivananda, "Brother, can you make a gift of this young man to me?"

Swami Shivananda replied, "Certainly you can have him! He is at your disposal."

Then Swami Brahmananda said, "He is a good young man. I'll make him my disciple." It needs to be mentioned here that Swami Brahmananda wouldn't easily agree to make anyone his disciple. Only after a careful examination would he agree. With his saintly insight he must have seen the spiritual potential of Suren. That's why he wanted to have Suren as his disciple. After a few days Suren was given spiritual initiation by Swami Brahmananda. Eventually he joined the Order as a monk, and after taking his final vows of sannyasa became known as Swami Nirvedananda.

I heard the above story from Swami Bodhatmananda.

Swami Nirvedananda passed away about four decades ago, but the Order still remembers him as a great educator and a most loving and saintly soul. Once, in Belur Math, Swami Gambhirananda said to some of us, "Had Swami Nirvedananda been still alive, he would have made an excellent President of our Order."

SWAMI JAGADANANDA—AN EXEMPLARY MONK

Swami Jagadananda (1879–1951) was a disciple of the Holy Mother Sri Sarada Devi. In his premonastic life he had been married and had worked as a teacher in the Government High School in Shillong. Once he went to hear a discourse given by someone on *The Gospel of Sri Ramakrishna*. In the *Gospel* Sri Ramakrishna was talking about the necessity for renunciation in spiritual life. These words inspired him immensely, and he eventually joined the Ramakrishna Order as a monk. While in the Order, he gained a high level of spirituality through

SWAMI JAGADANANDA
(1879–1951)

intense spiritual practice.

The Holy Mother Sri Sarada Devi said about him: "He is a *yogabhrashta rishi* (a saintly soul who died before experiencing God in his previous incarnation)."

The swami was grave and serious by nature and usually liked to remain immersed in his own thoughts. But he was well-versed in the scriptures and would happily accommodate those who would come to discuss scriptural topics with him. Though erudite, he lacked scholastic vanity.

Once some pundits came to him for a scriptural discussion. During the discussion, they entered into a debate with the swami and raised some objections regarding the interpretation of a certain text. Swami Jagadananda politely refuted the objections. Then the pundits thanked the swami and left.

But their scholarly vanity had been hurt. After two or three days they came again and said to the swami, "Sir, we've come to have some more scriptural discussion with you." This time they came well prepared to prove their intellectual superiority. Swami Jagadananda could guess their intent. He folded his hands in salutation to them and replied, "You're all most welcome here, but there's no need for any more scriptural discussion. I admit that you won in our previous discussion and I lost."

I heard from Swami Bodhatmananda the unusual story about how Swami Jagadananda was initiated by the Holy Mother Sri Sarada Devi. His initiation took place before he became a monk. He and a close friend of his went to the Holy Mother and prayed for spiritual initiation. The Holy Mother took Swami Jagadananda aside and said to him, "My child, both you and your friend were together in your past incarnation. This time also you've come together. In your last incarnation your friend was your guru and you were his disciple. To be initiated by me, you have to take his permission first."

Swami Jagadananda asked his friend for permission, but apparently to tease Swami Jagadananda, he wouldn't permit him immediately. He, however, gave his permission after a little while.

Then the Holy Mother initiated both of them. After the initiation, she said to Swami Jagadananda, "You used to be a *rishi* before (a saintly soul in the past incarnation), and again you've become one!"

Swami Pranavatmananda told us some of his reminiscences of Swami Jagadananda that I record below:

"The Swami Jagadananda I knew was an extremely loving and affectionate monk. Outwardly he appeared to be very reserved and grave, but his heart overflowed with love and compassion. When I joined Belur Math as a monk, I was quite young. Shortly thereafter I had to go somewhere with Swami Jagadananda by train. The journey was to last nearly three hours. The coach that we entered was packed with passengers. Swami Jagadananda was able to get some sitting space, but I had to stand. Then Swami Jagadananda asked me to sit on his lap. I vehemently protested, but in spite of my protestations he persuaded me to sit on his lap for all three hours until we arrived at our destination. This is just one example of how he felt for the junior brother monks.

"Another example. I was then traveling with Swami Jagadananda in Kashmir. We were on a pilgrimage and had to walk many miles in extremely cold weather. As a result, my arms seemed to lose much of their strength. They developed severe pain and I could no longer lift them any higher than my shoulders. This worried Swami Jagadananda very much. We were traveling in a very sparsely populated, mountainous region of Kashmir. The swami procured some medicinal oil for rheumatism, and also some tiger fat (considered good for relieving muscular aches) from the villagers. Then he started massaging my arms and shoulders with them. In our Order the junior monks are expected to serve their senior brothers; they are not supposed to accept service from their seniors. So I repeatedly said to Swami Jagadananda, "Maharaj, you needn't massage me, let me help myself." But he wouldn't listen to me. He massaged my arms regularly for a few days until I was cured.

"I find it hard to forget the love and affection that I got from him. In those days our monasteries served the simplest food. Milk was a rare item on our menu. Once in a while senior monks were given a cup of milk during dinner. One day I was sitting next to Swami Jagadananda in the dining hall. When he was given a cup of milk he immediately passed it on to me and forced me to drink it. Even though he was always eager to serve others, he himself didn't like to accept service from others.

"He was of a meditative temperament, but I never saw him formally sitting down and meditating in the daytime. When visitors or monks came to see him he would talk to them normally. But as soon as they left, he would close his eyes and become absorbed in meditation. If someone else would come to see him, he would then open his eyes and talk to him as much as was necessary. When that person too would leave, he would again close his eyes and enter into a meditative mood. This is how he went on meditating intermittently throughout the entire day. About him Swami Shivananda commented, 'He is one who has had the experience of samadhi.'

"The story of how he passed away is also wonderful. Shortly before his death, the unbearable pain he was experiencing made him lose consciousness for some time. Later regaining consciousness, like a true advaitin he started saying loudly, 'I am not the body, the vital energy, the mind or the senses… etc.' At the end he said, 'Aham Brahmasmi (I am Brahman)!' Then he passed away."

SOME REMINISCENCES ABOUT SWAMI SHUDDHANANDA

Swami Madhavananda, the ninth President of our Order, once said about Swami Shuddhananda, "He was my friend, guide and philosopher."

I already knew that Swami Shuddhananda, also known in our Order as Sudhir Maharaj, was the fifth President of our Order, and one of the most exalted disciples of Swami Vivekananda. I also knew that he had translated Swami Vivekananda's *Rajayoga, Karmayoga, Bhaktiyoga, Jnanayoga* and many other books into Bengali. His excellent translations fully retained the beauty and grandeur of the original English texts. Nevertheless, Swami Madhavananda's words made me eager to know more about Swami Shuddhananda as a person. I wanted

SWAMI SHUDDHANANDA
(1872–1938)

to know what he looked like, how he behaved with others, etc. I was then a junior monk living in Belur Math. Fortunately, I came to know some senior monks living in Belur Math who had known Swami Shuddhananda. I thought that they might be able to satisfy my curiosity. One of them was Swami Gangeshananda.

So I went to Swami Gangeshananda and said, "Please tell me about Swami Shuddhananda, Please tell me how he looked."

Swami Gangeshananda gave an objective description: "He was of medium height, fair-complexioned, and rather slim. He was slightly cross-eyed, and had a few birthmarks on his body."

"Please tell me about his nature. Was he very grave? Or was he easily approachable?" I asked.

Swami Gangeshananda replied, "Oh no, he wasn't that grave or anything. In fact, he was quite easy to approach. Everyone, young or old, could mix with him freely. One of his extraordinary qualities was his straightforwardness and frankness. But his frankness would sometimes create minor complications for others. Many years ago, Swami Brahmananda, our first President, was visiting our Kankhal sevashrama. When he would visit the branch ashramas, like the one in Kankhal, he would always donate money to them. Many devotees would come to see him when he would visit these ashramas, and often stayed to have their meals there. Thus, the expenses of the ashramas would temporarily mount. Swami Brahmananda's donations were meant to relieve the financial strain.

"Swami Kalyanananda, the head of the Kankhal sevashrama, casually mentioned to Swami Shuddhananda that the money Swami Brahmananda gave was not enough to meet the deficit caused by his visit. Swami Shuddhananda, in a frank way, artlessly told Swami Brahmananda what Swami Kalyanananda had said. As a result Swami Brahmananda immediately asked for an almanac, and consulted it to find the earliest, and most auspicious time, to leave Kankhal. Hearing this, Swami Kalyanananda rushed to Swami Brahmananda, fell at this feet, and begged him again and again not to leave. Then Swami Brahmananda changed his mind.

"Swami Shuddhananda's lifestyle was extremely austere. The only luxury he indulged in was having two or three smokes a day. He used to smoke Bidis, the most inexpensive handmade little cigars available in India.[9] One packet of Bidis at that time would only cost about eight or ten cents. But he had no money and often found it hard to buy them. One day he went for a visit to Udbodhan (a publication center of the Ramakrishna Order) where Swami Saradananda, the Secretary of the Ramakrishna Order, used to live. Swami Shuddhananda said to Swami Saradananda, 'I've translated all these books of Swamiji (Swami Vivekananda), but such is my fate that I can't even get money to buy two or three Bidis a day!'

---

9. Use of liquor or other intoxicants is strictly prohibited in the Ramakrishna Order. Only smoking of tobacco is permitted, but not encouraged.

"Hearing this, Swami Saradananda called Ganen Maharaj (a monk who helped Swami Saradananda) and said, 'From now on I'll give Prabhu (Swami Shuddhananda's nickname) five rupees a month.'"

Some years later, another incident happened. Swami Shuddhananda was then the General Secretary of the Order. At that time Tarasar Pundit used to give scriptural classes to the junior monks in Belur Math. One day the pundit got involved in a scriptural discussion with Swami Shuddhananda. The discussion gradually heated up and the pundit lost control of himself. He angrily said something improper to Swami Shuddhananda. Next morning he came to realize his mistake and thought, "In a fit of anger I've insulted Swami Shuddhananda, the General Secretary of the Order. After this incident they won't allow me to stay here anymore!" So thinking, he quietly was getting ready to leave bag and baggage.

Just then Swami Shuddhananda was going past the pundit's room. Taking out a Bidi from his shirt pocket, he offered it to the pundit and said, "Pundit, have a smoke." The swami was not the least bit affected by the insulting words of Tarasar Pundit. In fact, he had totally forgotten his unpleasant behavior. Such was Swami Shuddhananda!

Like his guru, Swami Vivekananda, Swami Shuddhananda was endowed with a photographic memory. In this connection Swami Sambuddhananda told us a very interesting story. It was in the year 1936, the year of the birth-centenary of Sri Ramakrishna. The Order decided to observe Sri Ramakrishna's birth-anniversary that year on a grand scale. Swami Akhandananda, the President of the Order, was requested to write an article about Sri Ramakrishna, to be circulated all over the world through the Order's branches. But Swami

Akhandananda said, "Sri Ramakrishna was Divinity itself; he was beyond birth and death. The idea of his birth-centenary is ridiculous. I won't write anything." Swami Sambuddhananda was the secretary of the centenary committee. He tried in so many ways to persuade Swami Akhandananda to write the article, but he wouldn't do it.

Then Swami Sambuddhananda went to Swami Shuddhananda for his advice. Swami Shuddhananda said that since Swami Akhandananda was reluctant to contribute an article, Swami Vivekananda's statements about Sri Ramakrishna should be collected from his lectures and put together. That would make a nice article about Sri Ramakrishna. Then Swami Shuddhananda quoted from memory the page numbers, paragraphs, and volume numbers from *The Complete Works of Swami Vivekananda* (it had eight volumes at that time), where such statements could be found. Swami Sambuddhananda, who noted down all the particulars, was astounded by this extraordinary memory power of Swami Shuddhananda. The article, however, didn't have to be used, because Swami Akhandananda later changed his mind and wrote an article about Sri Ramakrishna.

Now I would like to conclude by telling another story displaying a different aspect of Swami Shuddhananda's wonderful personality. Any sincere spiritual aspirant knows how difficult it is to meditate properly. Until the mind has come under control to a considerable extent and gained a certain level of purity, it is not possible to meditate properly. Chanting the holy name of God, regular study of the scriptures, etc., gradually enable the mind to meditate properly. And when meditation matures it becomes samadhi.

In those days there were not that many junior monks living in Belur Math. Therefore, most of them helped in doing various chores around the monastery. One morning when the monks were busy cutting vegetables in the kitchen, Swami Brahmananda said to them, "Each of you peel a potato, and then bring all of them together to me. Seeing them I'll be able to tell who among you can really meditate."

The monks peeled the potatoes, put them on a platter, and brought it to Swami Brahmananda. Glancing only once at the platter, Swami Brahmananda pointed at a particular potato and said, "The one who has peeled this potato is the only one who can meditate properly." That potato had been peeled by Swami Shuddhananda.

THE SOOTHING TOUCH OF HOLINESS

Swami Vishuddhananda (1883–1962) was then the Vice-President of our Order. Once the queen of a Himalayan kingdom came to Belur Math to see him, because she had heard of the swami's holiness, even in her country. Upon arrival, she prayed for a private interview with the swami and it was granted. Entering Swami Vishuddhananda's room, she closed the door behind her, saluted the swami, and sat down. She didn't say a single word, just sat there and shed tears silently for quite sometime. Then composing herself she said, "'Swamiji, now my mind is at peace. At home there's no place where I can empty the bottled-up pain in my heart. In your presence I've found peace. Please bless me."

She sat in front of Swami Vishuddhananda for a while without saying a word. Then saluting the swami with great devotion, she quietly left the room.

SOME REMINISCENCES ABOUT SWAMI OMKARANANDA

SWAMI OMKARANANDA
(1896–1973)

A swami in his late sixties had come to attend a monthly meeting of the trustees in Belur Math. He had come from the Order's branch at Kankurgachhi in Calcutta. He was a trustee of the Math and the head of the Kankurgachhi branch. As the center didn't have a car, a devotee drove the swami in his car to Belur Math. After the meeting, the same devotee's car was to take the swami back to the ashrama.

A young brahmachari named Mihir was going that day to the Shillong ashrama from Belur Math. In order to go to Shillong, which is several hundred miles away from Belur Math, he had to catch a train at Sealdah Railroad Station. Sealdah is around seven miles from Belur Math, and on the way to Kankurgachhi. The swami came to know of this, and asked the brahmachari to get into the car with his baggage. After arriving at the Sealdah Railroad Station, the car was parked and the trunk opened. The swami pulled out the brahmachari's baggage, hoisted it onto his own shoulder, and began walking quickly toward the railroad station. Brahmachari Mihir, even though in good health, was quite skinny. It seems that's why the swami didn't want him to carry his heavy baggage. Mihir felt extremely embarrassed. He begged, "Maharaj, please give me the baggage. I'll carry it." But the swami wouldn't listen to him. He carried the baggage all the way to the departure lounge of the railroad station. This swami was Swami Omkarananda. He later became a Vice-President of our Order.

In our Order junior monks are not supposed to receive this kind of service from monks who are senior to them in monastic life, or who are older in age. That's why the brahmachari felt so embarrassed. This incident shows Swami Omkarananda's total lack of false ego, in addition to his loving concern for the younger brother monks.

Swami Omkarananda was endowed with many wonderful qualities. Besides being an exemplary monk, he was a man of great scholarship. His command over the traditional Hindu scriptures was phenomenal. He had studied them exhaustively under famous pundits when he had lived in Varanasi. He also had thoroughly studied Western philosophy and various non-Hindu religions. In spite of his great erudition, he was never interested in writing books. Swami Omkarananda was also one of those monks in our Order who were adepts in ritualistic worship.

An incident happened when Swami Shivananda was the President of our Order. Swami Shivananda was a God-realized soul. Although he would try to hide his high spiritual stature from others, it would sometimes accidentally be revealed. An astrologer once came to tell his future. Some other monks were present at the time. After some calculations the astrologer said to Swami Shivananda, "Maharaj, you will experience Brahman (God)."

With childlike simplicity Swami Shivananda said, "Why do you say I will experience Brahman? Say that I've already experienced Brahman."[10]

Even though Swami Shivananda had experienced Brahman, he was not a scholar of the scriptures. Once a pundit came to see Swami Shivananda. He said to the swami, "Maharaj, I would like to have a scriptural discussion with you."

Swami Omkarananda, then a young monk, was present there. He said to the pundit, "If you want to know about Brahman, ask him. But if you want to have a scriptural discussion, you can have that with me."

As mentioned earlier, Swami Omkarananda had great love for his younger brother monks. He himself was inspired by the life and teachings of Swami Vivekananda, and expected the younger monks to be inspired likewise. He expected the junior monks to be mentally and spiritually strong, and completely dedicated to the spiritual ideal. He also wanted them to study the traditional Hindu scriptures, in addition to the works of Swami Vivekananda.

Romain Rolland of France once asked Rabindranath Tagore, the Nobel Prize winner poet of India, "How can I know India?"

Tagore replied, "Read Vivekananda. In him everything is positive, nothing negative." The same statement can be applied to Swami Omkarananda. In him everything was positive, nothing negative. His youthful mind was always eager to know newer truths and explore newer dimensions of knowledge. For example, in his seventies he became interested in learning about Indian classical music.

One notable characteristic of Swami Omkarananda was his

---

10. The astrologer said in Hindi, "Maharaj, apka Brahmajnan hoga." Swami Shivananda replied in Hindi, "Hoga kniu? Bolo, 'Ho goya.'"

total lack of interest in maintaining an external image. Once a middle-aged gentleman came to Belur Math from Singapore. He had come all the way from Singapore just to see Swami Om-karananda. The gentleman had once met the swami when he had visited Singapore several years earlier. The gentleman was staying as a guest in Belur Math. Swami Gambhirananda, the General Secretary, asked me to accompany him to our Kankurgachhi ashrama where he would meet Swami Omkarananda. Swami Omkarananda was at that time the Vice-President of our Order.

After having breakfast at Belur Math, we arrived in Kankur-gachhi by car early in the morning. Swami Omkarananda had just come out of the temple after finishing his meditation. Then he sat on the veranda next to his office, and was served breakfast on a rickety coffee table. The breakfast consisted of some cut fruits that had been offered to the Deity. We were asked to sit on the veranda while the swami ate his breakfast.

As soon as he had finished eating, he took out his dentures and put them on a plate in front of him. He didn't care in the least whether the visiting gentleman would consider his behavior strange, and not in conformity with the expected behavior of the Vice-President of a global religious Order. Then Swami Omkarananda started talking animatedly about spiritual matters. The gentleman sat there and silently listened to every word of the swami with rapt attention. His eyes sparkled with admiration for the swami. The meeting lasted about an hour. On our way back to Belur Math, the gentleman remarked, "I have no doubts that Swami Omkarananda is a genuine saint. He is not the least conscious of his image or what people think of him. He is a Vedantic lion fearlessly roaming in the forest of this world!" I was touched by his great regard for Swami Omkarananda.

⧗ WORK IS WORSHIP

SWAMI MADHAVANANDA
(1888–1965)

In the beginning a spiritual aspirant both works *and* worships. Then he learns to do his work *as* worship. Eventually he gains the conviction that work *is* worship.

Swami Nirjarananda, also known as Mohit Maharaj (1916–2002), was then the manager of the Calcutta Advaita ashrama. The following incident occurred on one occasion when he had come to Belur Math to discuss some important matter with the General Secretary, Swami Madhavananda:

Swami Madhavananda was very regular in his habits. Every evening after sunset, he would close the door of his room and meditate for two hours. At that time nobody was supposed to disturb him. Swami Nirjarananda arrived at Belur Math just after sunset, and found the door of Swami Madhavananda's room closed. So he decided to wait outside the door until the swami finished his meditation. After two hours the door was opened, and he entered Swami Madhavananda's room, saluted him, and explained why he had come to see him.

Swami Madhavananda then said to Swami Nirjarananda (Mohit Maharaj), "Mohit, in the future if you have to see me in connection with any business that's as urgent as this, don't hesitate to push the door open and enter my room. You can disturb me even if I'm meditating. To me there's no difference between work and worship."

Holy Mother Sri Sarada Devi once praised the spiritual potential of young Swami Madhavananda saying, "He is as precious as the tusk of an elephant plated with gold." Swami Madhavananda, a karma yogi par excellence, later became the ninth President of the Ramakrishna Order.

While he was the General Secretary, Swami Madhavananda for a while suffered from a severe attack of eczema. The eczema gradually developed a weeping character and spread all over his legs. It was no longer possible for him to work at his desk sitting on his chair. But that didn't stop him from doing his usual work. With his legs stretched out on a freshly cut banana leaf, he would sit in his office and go on working as usual. Unfortunately, for years no medicine was of any help, until the new drug hydrocortisone became available in India. This medicine cured Swami Madhavananda's skin problem.

At the General Secretary's office there was an orderly named Tewari. He had worked there for many years. Once he said to a senior swami, "I've been working here in Belur Math for a long time but I have never seen a monk as exalted as Swami Madhavananda."

Another exemplary swami of our Order for whom work had become worship was Swami Diptananda (1897–1989), popularly known as Prabodh Maharaj. He spent his entire monastic life working in the flower room of the Sri Ramakrishna Temple at Belur Math.

When I first saw him nearly forty years ago, he must have been in his early sixties. He was still physically fit and working every day from dawn till late in the evening—as long as the temple remained open. The marble floor of the temple was very cold in the winter months. He had to work barefooted all the time. As a result, he started suffering from occasional pains in his legs. Due to the traditional austere lifestyle practiced in the monastery, the monks of Belur Math didn't wear socks. Swami Vishuddhananda, the Vice-President of the Order, heard about Prabodh Maharaj's leg pains and provided him with warm socks to protect his feet from the cold.

When we were brahmacharis at the Probationers' Training Center at Belur Math, we occasionally worked in the flower room of the temple under the supervision of Prabodh Maharaj. It was part of our training program. Prabodh Maharaj was very strict, and scolded us severely if we made mistakes. He was a perfectionist, and expected us to give the best service to Sri Ramakrishna. In spite of his scolding, I developed great respect for him.

Many religious festivals are held in Belur Math. During those frequent festivals, elaborate ritualistic worships are performed in the temple. As a result, the work in the flower room increases substantially. Prabodh Maharaj managed all that work with the utmost dedication. He had the help of one or two assistants.

His daily routine was to get up from bed before 4 o'clock in the morning. After taking a shower, he would meditate for a while and then go to the temple before 5 a.m. to help the *puja-ri* (the monk who did the worship) perform *mangalarati* (early morning worship). It was his habit to silently chant the holy name of God while working in the flower room. He would speak only when necessary. Late in the morning he would begin arranging for the midday worship, before the pujari came to perform it.

Preparation for this worship was pretty elaborate. Two kinds of sandalwood paste had to be made. Many flowers were used for the worship. Each and every flower had to be rinsed to make it perfectly clean and free from insects. Durba grass (a special kind of grass used for worship), vilwa leaves and basil leaves had to be made ready for use in the worship. Prabodh Maharaj made sure that each blade of grass was perfect, and every leaf was fresh and clean. Water, fruits, sweets, and various cooked dishes were offered to the Deity.

After the midday worship the temple would be closed. Then Prabodh Maharaj would eat lunch and rest for an hour or two. When the temple reopened around 3 p.m., he again went to the flower room and prepared the refreshments that were offered to the Deity at that time. Around dusk he had to make all arrangements for the evening *arati* (vespers). After arati, he would prepare for the evening food offering to the Deity. By the time the food offering was over, it would be around 9 p. m. Then the temple would be closed for the night. Prabodh Maharaj would then have his supper and go to sleep. Day in and day out, year after year, he followed this routine like an untiring clock.

He very rarely went on a vacation. In his seventies, with the permission of the headquarters, he went on a vacation to one of our village ashramas in Bengal. He was supposed to spend a month there. But he returned to Belur Math after only a few days. When asked why he had returned so early he replied, "I missed serving Thakur (the Lord) in our temple." Never again did he go on a vacation.

Prabodh Maharaj was one of those unsung heroes of our Order who never cared for creature comforts, power or position. The very nature of his work kept Prabodh Maharaj away from the limelight. Outsiders rarely noticed him. Yet, throughout his entire monastic life, he silently and lovingly served God. And through this service, he transformed his work into worship.

🏛 WHAT MONKS LIVE BY

Many retired elderly monks live in Belur Math. During their active years, all of them did a lot of philanthropic work. In their old age I used to see them leading a more or less colorless life in Belur Math. I saw them doing their morning and evening meditations, and having three monotonous meals a day. Sometimes I would see them sitting on the benches on the veranda of the monks' quarters reading the daily newspapers. Otherwise, they would be in their rooms reading some religious books, or replying to letters they had received. I didn't notice anything spectacular in their lifestyle. I was young in monastic life, and often wondered what had sustained them through all those years of monastic life.

Around that time a senior brother monk gave me some very valuable advice. He said, "If you want to find joy in monastic life try to give personal service to our elderly brother monks." I followed his advice and started getting great joy out of it. At first the elderly monks protested, and wouldn't allow me to give them any personal service. Nevertheless, I would sometimes secretly take their soiled clothes and wash them. After drying the clothes in the sun, I would fold them neatly and put them back in their rooms. Gradually they came to know what I was doing and stopped protesting. They came to accept my service with loving indulgence. And then they would sometimes reveal to me what inspired them to become monks.

Hidden inside their hearts were caskets holding invaluable gems. Those gems were the words of inspiration from their gurus. Once in a while they would open their hearts and talk about their gurus. As they spoke, their faces would light up with a rare kind of beauty. This beauty can only be seen in people fired by high idealism. Seeing them, I felt that I must never leave them. I also felt that if heaven existed anywhere on earth, it was where they were. I came to learn that it is this idealism that had sustained them through all those years of their monastic life. It is what they lived by.

⧗ HOW TO KNOW IF THE HEALTH OF A MONK IS ALL RIGHT 1892 – 1985

Swami Vireswarananda (1916–1978) was then the General Secretary of the Ramakrishna Order. He lived in Belur Math in one of the rooms of the office building that housed the headquarters of the Ramakrishna Order. I was a young monk working in that office. It was the time when many were suffering from flu. Unfortunately, Swami Vireswarananda, who was in his early seventies, contracted the illness and had to be in bed for two or three days. As soon as his temperature went down, he started working full time in his office. Around that time Swami Vishwashrayananda, the head of our Udbodhan ashrama in Calcutta, came to see him. After saluting Swami Vireswarananda he asked, "Are you all right Maharaj? I heard that you were ill with flu."

With a smile on his face Swami Vireswarananda responded to the query saying, "Do you know how to judge if a monk is ill or well?"

Swami Vishwashrayananda replied tactfully, "Maharaj, please tell me how to judge it."

Still smiling, Swami Vireswarananda said, "If you see the

monk lying in bed unable to even lift his head, know him to be ill. But if he can sit up on his bed, know him to be all right!"

I happened to be present in Swami Vireswarananda's office at that time and heard this interesting conversation. I understood that monks who have dedicated their lives to God should be prepared to serve Him in spite of minor illnesses as Swami Vireswarananda was then doing.

BROTHERLY LOVE—THE REAL CEMENTING FORCE OF THE RAMAKRISHNA ORDER

Swami Vishuddhananda, then the Vice-President of our Order, was visiting the Ramakrishna Mission Home of Service in Varanasi. Swami Bhaswarananda, the head of that ashrama, was very fond of Swami Vishuddhananda.

One day Swami Bhaswarananda came to Swami Vishuddhananda with a problem. It was about a newly joined pre-probationer monk of the ashrama. The monk had committed some offence deserving expulsion from the Order. Before asking him to leave, Swami Bhaswarananda thought it proper to seek the opinion of Swami Vishuddhananda, whom he respected highly. Swami Vishuddhananda said to Swami Bhaswarananda, "I understand that the monk has committed an offence. But should we not forgive him? Like us he also must have come to the Order because of his love of Sri Ramakrishna!"

Swami Bhaswarananda allowed the monk to stay. But after a while the monk left the Order on his own. Nevertheless, Swami Vishuddhananda repeatedly reminded us that the cementing force of our Order was the love between the brother monks. He also pointed out that such brotherly love can only be generated by our intense love of Sri Ramakrishna.

Part II

Having been in the company of numerous brother monks of our Order over the years, many times I have experienced that brotherly love that welds our hearts together. I narrate below an incident, which exemplifies that kind of love:

In 1974 the authorities in Belur Math asked me to go to our Seattle ashrama in the United States as assistant to Swami Vividishananda. Until then, for nearly eleven years, I had been working at the headquarters office in Belur Math. The day before my departure for Seattle, I went to all the senior brother monks in Belur Math and sought their blessings. Swami Vireswarananda was our Order's President at that time. As he was very busy in the daytime, I got permission to see him around 10:30 p.m. He was in his eighties then, and had lost much of his vision from a complication in his optic nerve. After I entered his room and saluted him, he gave me a lot of encouragement in regard to my new assignment abroad. Then he added, "I'll see you off when you depart from Belur Math."

But I was to take a very early morning flight. I needed to start from Belur Math before daybreak—around 4:30 a.m. So I said to him, "Maharaj, it is not necessary for you to come and see me off that early in the morning. Besides, it will be quite dark then. You'll have difficulty walking in the dark." I also knew that he wouldn't be able to go to bed that night before 11:30 p.m. If he had to see me off at 4:30 in the morning, he would hardly have time to sleep.

Next morning, as I was about to enter the car that would take me to the airport, my brother monks said, "Wait! President Maharaj (Swami Vireswarananda) is coming." He came walking very slowly, using his cane, while his attendant showed the way with a powerful flashlight.

I was only an insignificant junior monk, and he was the highly venerated President of our Order. Despite his poor eyesight and advanced age, he came to see me off in the dark hours of the morning. His love and compassion completely overwhelmed me. I bent low and saluted him. Then with tears welling up in my eyes and a heavy heart, I started for the airport. That day he set for me an unforgettable example of what selfless brotherly love should be. It is this love that binds all of us together in the Ramakrishna Order.

⧗ ONE WHO EXPERIENCED THE ATMAN

SWAMI ATULANANDA
(1870–1966)

It was March 15, 1958. A venerable 88 year-old monk was talking privately to a few younger brother monks about his spiritual experience. He was telling them how he once vividly experienced that he was divine and separate from this world. The world then appeared to him like a huge ball full of moving creatures, and he felt that he had no connection whatsoever with it. He said, "I am divine: that is perceived on a certain plane of consciousness. In the normal plane, however, I am here; these things are real, as dream objects appear to be real in the dream-state."

Again on March 16th he talked to his brother monks about the same experience, "When I experienced that the world, with all moving creatures, was entirely separate from me, like a ball, or like the planet Mars in the sky, I had no body consciousness, and I felt that I had no connection whatsoever with this world—neither had I any connection with it in the past, nor have I now, nor will I have in the future. And I found others also to be contained in the divine Atman, and thought: 'If only these people could know about it!' I found no desire in me—complete desirelessness. But still I had the idea of many Atmans. I didn't have that idea of Oneness, One in all."[11]

Then he continued, "Hari Maharaj (Swami Turiyananda) told me, 'First one has to know oneself; then one can know others to be the same.'

"Illumination comes suddenly, quickly. How and when, it cannot be said. When I learned bicycling, at first I couldn't maintain my balance. The teacher told me, 'Don't look at the wheel; look straight ahead.' Then suddenly it was all right. So you see, a teacher is needed. The knack comes suddenly."[12]

Swami Atulananda was that elderly monk. Highly respected in the Ramakrishna Order, he was popularly known as Gurudas Maharaj. He was a disciple of the Holy Mother Sri Sarada Devi and had been initiated into sannyasa by Swami Abhedananda in 1923. He was born in Holland in 1870, and he later immigrated to the United States. The last 44 years of his life he spent in India, until he passed away in 1966 at the age of 96. He had had the wonderful privilege of knowing all the monastic disciples of Sri Ramakrishna, except for Swami Yogananda and Swami Niranjanananda.

Gurudas Maharaj once went on a pilgrimage to Kedar-

11. *Atman Alone Abides* (Sri Ramakrishna Math, Madras), p. 27.
12. Ibid, 27.

nath and Badrinarayan, two famous holy places in the Himalayas, with three brother monks, including Swami Prabhavananda. In the temple in Badrinarayan, they had a very amazing experience, which I record below from Swami Prabhavananda's reminiscences published posthumously in the March 1979 issue of the *Prabuddha Bharata*.

SWAMI PRABHAVANANDA
(1893–1976)

"...Finally we arrived at Badrinarayan. All the pilgrims sat down, waiting for the temple to open. We too were seated to one side. A bright-looking young priest, about twenty to twenty-four years old beckoned to me. He said, 'Ask your friends to come and follow me.' He took us to a side of the temple where it was not crowded. When he opened the temple door, some other pilgrims wanted to enter also, but he told them: 'No, it is not for you.' The four of us went in with him, and he closed the door behind us. But here is the peculiar thing. Generally a priest stands to one side or in front, facing the deity. But this priest stood in line with the deity, facing us, which is never done. We stayed and had our *darshan* (view of the deity). After a few minutes, the priest asked: 'Have you had enough darshan?'

"We came out, but the priest did not leave the temple. He closed the door behind us. Again we were seated with the pilgrims. Another man beckoned to me. 'Ask your friends to come with me. The head priest wants to see you.'

"We went, and the head priest with great courtesy made us sit by him. He asked in Hindi about Gurudas Maharaj (Swami Atulananda), 'To what race does this man belong?'

"I knew a little Hindi, and I answered: 'You have no right to inquire about the race or caste of a monastic.'

"The head priest replied: 'I know, but does he not come from America?' He explained that he himself did not mind, but as Gurudas Maharaj looked white, other people would make trouble for him. If they saw him entering the temple, he would have to pay a large sum of money to have it purified. The head priest asked the three of us not to go into the temple either, as we ate with Gurudas Maharaj. But he was very kind to us. Every hour he would wave the aratrika lights (lights waved in front of the deity during worship) before the deity and would let us watch from the open temple door; at that time he would not permit other pilgrims to enter the temple. After we had our darshan he would allow the other pilgrims to go inside. We never told him or anyone else there that we had already been inside the temple.

"For three days and three nights the four of us were practically guests of the head priest. He arranged for our stay in a heated room and sent us the best prasad (consecrated food). There were about seven or eight priests at Badrinarayan, and we met them all; but we never saw the young priest again who had conducted us into the temple when we first arrived.

"From Badrinarayan, on the way back to Mayavati, Swami Raghavananda, Gurudas Maharaj and I stopped at Almora, where Swami Turiyananda was then staying in the Ramakrishna Kutir. We did not know where in Almora the Kutir was located. Although we had been told that it was somewhere beside the road, we happened to come to just the right place. I had begun to call loudly, 'Swami Turiyanandaji Maharaj, Swami Turiyanandaji Maharaj!'

"It was early morning. The swami had been warming himself by a fire, dressed only in a *kaupin* (loincloth). As soon as he heard my voice, he came running outside into the cold to meet me. Think of his love! Then he took me by the hand and led me to the Kutir, and Gurudas Maharaj and Swami Raghavananda also came. He gave us a warm welcome.

"We stayed with Swami Turiyananda for three days, and we told him the story of our pilgrimage. When he heard about our first darshan at Badrinarayan, when the young priest had taken us inside the temple, he became excited and exclaimed: 'You foolish boys, didn't you realize that it was the Lord Himself who came in this garb and took you inside? Didn't you recognize Him?'"

About Swami Atulananda, Swami Vidyatmananda of the Ramakrishna Order writes: "The one idea that sustained Gurudas Maharaj (Swami Atulananda) all through his life, including his last days when he suffered from a painful cancer near the eye, was the Vedantic doctrine—'I am the Atman. Everything else changes. The Atman alone abides.'"

Nearly three months before his passing away, Swami Atulananda had a serious heart attack at the Barlowganj ashrama where he was staying. Getting the news, Swami Dhireshananda and another monk from our hospital center in Kankhal immediately went to Barlowganj. They carried with them an oxygen cylinder to relieve the swami's breathing difficulty. The doctors gave various medicines, but the case seemed to be hopeless, the swami's age being against him. "Very weak, and the legs and face swollen, he could not even utter a few words. He had great difficulty in breathing. The end appeared imminent."[13] But Swami Atulananda greeted Swami Dhireshananda and his companion with a smile.

The next day Swami Dhireshananda and his companion had to return to Kankhal. They went to take leave of Gurudas Maharaj. Swami Dhireshananda writes: "We bowed before him and he laid his right hand on our heads quietly and blessed us. Lying on his left as he was, and raising his right hand a little, with much effort he said twice, 'The One is appearing as many.' This is perhaps our dear and revered Gurudas Maharaj's last expression of conviction. Thrilled, our eyes filled with tears. Slipping out of the room, we returned to Kankhal."

HUMAN CHANNELS OF DIVINE GRACE

Once a swami of our Order gave a mild scolding to one of his disciples. As a result, the devotee stopped coming to the ashrama for a while. The swami noticed it and inquired why the devotee hadn't been coming. Another devotee replied, "Maharaj, you are her guru. She is afraid to come because she made you angry."

The swami said, "Tell her that the one who became angry with her wasn't her guru. The guru can never be angry." What the swami meant was that he wasn't really the guru. God was the true guru. God used him as a channel to shower His grace on her. Aside from that, anger arises only when some obstacle is put in the path of the fulfillment of a desire. God lacks nothing

---

13. Ibid, 224.

SWAMI VIVIDISHANANDA
(1893–1980)

and has no unfulfilled desire. So God can never be angry.

Sri Ramakrishna used to say that God sometimes speaks through the mouths of little children or crazy people. God speaks through the mouths of holy people as well. The following incident about Swami Vividishananda of our Order, amply clarifies this point. A disciple of Swami Brahmananda, the swami was sent by our Order to the United States in 1929. After working as the head of the Vedanta Societies in Portland and San Francisco, he started a Vedanta center first in Washington D.C., and then in Denver. But both of them had to be closed down due to lack of popular interest. Then at the invitation of a small number of interested people, he came to Seattle in 1938, and founded a Vedanta Society there. Over the years the membership of the society gradually grew. The swami remained as its head until he passed away in 1980.

In 1974, when he was eighty years old, he had a stroke. After his recovery it was no longer possible for him to give Sunday lectures or conduct weekly classes at the society. In 1975 he had a second cerebral stroke. Around this time an incident happened. Let me quote below from the writing of a disciple of Swami Vividishananda, who witnessed the incident:

Part II

"He (Swami Vividishananda) had come home from the hospital and was being cared for by the monks, with some help from the devotees. But he did not recover, and could not even acknowledge people's presence. He could not talk normally, but instead would mutter indistinctly in, I think, Bengali (his mother tongue). He seemed to be living in an inner, invisible world. Still the devotees wanted to visit him, just to be in his company.

"One day after the swami had been given a shave, I went into his room simply to be in his presence. I was quite upset and sad about something, but had said nothing to the swami or anyone else about it. My presence was announced, but as usual there was no sign that the swami had heard. I thought I would just sit there quietly and find comfort in his presence. The swami was sitting limply, leaning back in his lounge chair, and muttering something indistinctly to himself.

"Then I was left alone in the room with the swami. I just sat quietly near him without saying a word.

"Suddenly Swami Vividishananda sat up in his chair, and in a clear, strong voice full of power, said in English, 'There is nothing in this world worth feeling bad about.' And then he sank limply back into his chair and began muttering away again indistinctly, apparently unaware of the outside world.

"His words had such an immense power that they went straight to my heart and never left. My heart completely lost its grief. And the words planted strength in my heart that has grown stronger through the years. Now I feel that it was the grace of God. God had used my guru, Swami Vividishananda, as the instrument to reach me."

⧗ SWAMI YATISWARANANDA'S ADVICE ON KARMAYOGA

SWAMI YATISWARANANDA
(1889–1966)

The junior monks used to come and pay their respects to Swami Yatiswarananda on special occasions. On one such occasion, after saluting the swami, they sat on the floor in front of him and said, "Maharaj (revered sir), please give us some advice for our spiritual life."

Thereupon Swami Yatiswarananda said, "I'll tell you about a lesson that I learnt when I was a young boy. One morning as I was going to school, I noticed a stray dog on the sidewalk with a bad sore on its body. We had some sulfur ointment at home and I knew that if the ointment were applied on the sore it would help the dog.

"So I went home, brought some ointment back and put it on the dog's sore. Then I went to school feeling happy, thinking that I had helped the dog and done a very good thing.

"After school, as I was walking back home, I saw the same dog on the sidewalk, but now the dog looked much sicker. It had vomited all over.

"Then I realized that in trying to help that poor dog, I had actually harmed it. Dogs have a natural tendency to lick their wounds. And that stray dog must have also licked its wound, and in so doing had swallowed the sulfur ointment that I had applied. Thus I learned that it's not enough to have a helping attitude. One must also know how to help properly.

"In the practice of Karmayoga we are expected to perform action with an unselfish attitude of mind. But that's not enough. We also have to know *how* to perform unselfish action properly and well."

Part III

More Reminiscences

SWAMI SHANTANANDA
by Swami Shantarupananda

I first met Swami Shantananda in 1963 when I was a college student. I had heard from others that he was a great spiritual soul of the Ramakrishna Order, and a disciple of the Holy Mother Sri Sarada Devi. I was also very much intrigued to hear that his *kundalini* had been awakened and that he would constantly hear the *anahata dhwani,* the sacred mystical sound *Om.* According to our scriptures, this sound can only be heard by spiritually illumined souls.

I first met him in a small room in the Premananda Memorial Building, which is across from the Swami Vivekananda Temple in Belur Math. He was sitting on a canvas reclining chair facing the river Ganga with a smiling face. His eyes were like the eyes of a bird hatching its eggs. His vision was half outward, half inward! I sat on a mat on the floor in front of him. He remained silent and withdrawn, and yet his presence radiated peace. I was so impressed that I kept on coming again and again to see him whenever I could get the time and opportunity. Gradually, as a result of those visits, I acquired enough courage to sometimes disturb his habitual silence and converse with him.

As mentioned earlier, I heard that Swami Shantananda could hear the anahata dhwani—the sound OM—all the time as a result of his incessant chanting of the holy name of God. The Holy Mother had asked him to continuously chant the mantra by saying, "Japat siddhih." ("One can have spiritual enlightenment by the chanting of the holy name of God alone.")

So I asked him one day, "Do you hear the sound Om now?"

He replied, "Yes, it started in 1911 in Varanasi. I was in that city for forty years. One night I began hearing the sacred Om sound. I thought this experience must be common to all; surely everyone hears it. From then onward I heard it all the time. Later I asked Swami Turiyananda. He told me that my kundalini had become awakened. He encouraged me."

I asked Swami Shantananda, "What does it sound like?"

Then he made the sound, a prolonged sound of Om.

"Maharaj, do you hear the sacred sound all the time?"

"Yes."

"Can you hear it when you are talking to me?"

"Even when I am talking, I'm aware that it's going on inside me. When I stop talking, I clearly hear the sound."

One day he was narrating his experiences about the Holy Mother, "We three (Swami Vishuddhananda, later the President of the Order; Swami Girijananda; and Swami Shantananda) went to Jayrambati together. The Holy Mother asked me, 'Do you want to take diksha (spiritual initiation)?'

"I replied, 'I don't know, Mother.'

"Nevertheless, she was very pleased. Among the three of us she initiated me first. We wanted to go on a pilgrimage all over India on foot. But she did not allow us. She said that it would be too hard. But she allowed us to go to Varanasi on foot. So we walked all the way from Jayrambati to Varanasi."

I asked, "Maharaj, didn't you have any difficulties on the way?"

"No, with the Holy Mother's blessings we had no difficulty on the way."

I already knew that those three great swamis of our Order were given gerua (ochre) cloth by the Holy Mother, and that she had asked them to go to Varanasi to get sannyasa names from Swami Shivananda. But it was, indeed, inspiring to hear the story directly from Swami Shantananda.

Illumined souls transcend their physical limitations. They don't care about food, shelter, or how old their bodies are. Their life-music is centered on God and God alone, nothing else. One day, I asked him, "Maharaj, how old are you?"

But he did not know his own age! He got embarrassed, just like a little boy. He called the monk who was his attendant, "Sushil, how old am I?"

The attendant, after much calculation, informed him, "You are now 84 years old."

Swami Shantananda was very happy to know his age. Then he turned towards me and said, "My age is now 84." Of course, I already had heard it!

Two years later I asked him again, "Maharaj, how old are you now?"

He replied without any hesitation, "My age is 84." As if his age would never change! I couldn't control my laughter.

Though he was totally oblivious of his chronological age, he was extremely alert about spiritual matters. Let me narrate one incident to illustrate this. I used to go to him in the afternoon almost every day, and he would invariably ask me to read aloud some pages from the book *Sri Sri Ramakrishna Kathamrita* (the original Bengali version of *The Gospel of Sri Ramakrishna*). As usual, one day sitting on a mat on the floor and facing the north, I was reading from the *Kathamrita*. And he was sitting on his canvas reclining chair silently facing the east, without saying a word. I had no way of knowing whether he was listening to the reading or was absorbed in his own holy thoughts. After I had read for quite a while, I suspected that most probably he was not listening to the reading. In order to test his attention, I deliberately omitted one Bengali word from the sentence I was reading. Immediately, he turned his head towards me and asked, "What did you read?" I was so embarrassed. I had to read the complete sentence all over again!

The *Kathamrita* has nearly 1,400 pages. Swami Shantananda apparently had got the entire book by heart. Just imagine, what a tremendous memory and what concentration! No wonder it is mentioned in our scriptures that those who are 100% celibate develop extraordinary memory.

Those who live with God always remember God in whatever they do. The proof of this I got in the life of Swami Shantananda. Once I made an enlargement of a photograph of Swami Shantananda and brought it to him. He looked at it intently, as if he was seeing someone else's picture.

I asked him, "Maharaj, do you like the photograph?"

He replied, "Yes, it is a good picture. But it looks so old."

I laughed. He was then 82 years old. Then I said, "Maharaj, will you kindly put your autograph on this picture?"

"Why my autograph?" he asked.

Somehow I mustered enough courage to tell him, "Maharaj, you got so many blessings from Holy Mother. Will you not give this small blessing to me?"

He was pleased and said, "All right, do you want me to write in Bengali or in English?"

I gladly replied, "Whatever you want, Maharaj."

Then he took a piece of paper and wrote something on it. I couldn't imagine what he was doing. I had requested him to give his autograph on his photo, not on a piece of paper! After writing something on the paper, he saluted it by touching it to his forehead. Then he wrote in English on the back of the picture, "Swami Shantananda, 22.3.66, (March 22, 1966)," and handed it over to me.

I was naturally curious to know what he had written on the paper. I picked it up and saw that he had written: *Shri Shri Ramakrishnah Sharanam,* which means *Shri Ramakrishna is my refuge.*

Prior to his passing away, his body became very emaciated, and he had a lot of ailments that come with old age. He was admitted to our hospital in Calcutta, the Ramakrishna Mission Seva Pratishthan. I went to see him in the hospital.

The moment I entered his room, I was shocked to see so many pieces of medical equipment surrounding his bed. A feeding tube had been inserted into his throat through his nose. On one side of his bed there was an oxygen cylinder. On the other side, I noticed some other medical equipment. The whole sight was shocking to me! But as soon as my eyes fell on his face all my anxieties evaporated. What a peaceful, serene face! The doctor came. He wanted to give him an injection. Swami Shantananda turned on his side. After injecting him, the doctor asked, "Maharaj, did you feel any pain?"

With a smile on his serene face he shook his head to indicate that he hadn't felt any pain.

Swami Shantananda passed away on Thursday, January 17, 1974, while chanting the name of the Divine Mother. His body was brought to Belur Math and put in his bedroom in the Premananda Memorial Building. It appeared as though Swami Shantananda had just fallen asleep. His face still retained its serene and peaceful expression.

The monks, devotees, and friends came to pay their last homage to him. One after another they came and saluted the swami. I was standing inside the room in a corner. Swami Abhayananda (Bharat Maharaj), another disciple of the Holy Mother, came in. He was a staunch advaitin. As a matter of principle, he wouldn't even salute a deity in a temple. That day we saw him slowly enter Swami Shantananda's room. Then with obvious feelings that he couldn't suppress, he folded his hands, saluted his dear and beloved brother-monk, and quietly walked out of the room.

Glossary

Advaitin: One who believes in the non-dual aspect of God.

Aham Brahmasmi: This expression literally means "I am Brahman (God)."

Anahata Dhwani: A sound that is not produced by any vibration in the atmosphere. Only advanced yogis or spiritual aspirants can hear this sound with their mental ears.

Arati: Vespers.

Aratrikam: Same as "Arati."

Atman: The indwelling Divine Self.

Atyutkata Karma: A very heinous action such as killing a woman or a holy person.

Bhairavi: A nun belonging to the spiritual discipline of Tanta.

Bhakti-Yoga: The Path of Love; one of the four fundamental types of spiritual disciplines helpful to experience the Ultimate Reality or Divinity.

Brahmachari: A novice in a monastery, or one who has taken the first vows of monastic life.

Brahmacharya: The first vows of monastic life. Also means celibacy.

Brahman: God, the Ultimate Divine Reality. The word literally means "greater than the greatest."

Brahmajnani: A knower of Brahman (God).

Chuddar: A wrapper made of cloth, silk or wool.

Darshan: Literally means "seeing." Also means spiritual vision.

Dhoti: A long piece of cloth used in India, Sri Lanka and Pakistan to cover the body from the waist down to the heels.

Diksha: Spiritual initiation.

Ganga: One of the rivers of India that are considered holy by the Hindus.

Gangasagar: The confluence of the river Ganga and the Bay of Bengal.

Ghat: A staircase built on the bank of a river or the shore of a lake leading to the deeper levels of water.

Hari Bol: This expression literally means "chant the name of Hari (God)."

Jivanmukta: One who has become liberated while alive.

Jnana-Yoga: The Path of Reasoning or Knowledge; one of the four fundamental types of spiritual disciplines to experience the Ultimate Reality or Divinity.

Karma: The word literally means "action." It also means the doctrine based on the idea that every doer has to experience the effects of his or her past actions.

Karma-Yoga: The Path of Right Action; one of the four fundamental types of spiritual disciplines that lead to the experience of the Ultimate Reality or Divinity.

Karma-Yogi: One who practices Karma Yoga.

Kaupin: Loincloth. Usually used by Hindu monks.

Kundalini: The spiritual power that lies dormant at the base of the backbone of every individual. This power can be awakened by intense spiritual practice.

Kutir: A cottage.

Lord Narayana: Lord Vishnu.

Maharaj: In the context of monastic life the word means a "holy man." When used to address a holy man, it means "Revered Sir."

Mantra: A holy name of God.

Math: A monastery where monks live.

Mela: A fair.

Naishthik Brahmachari: One avowed to lead the life of a Brahmachari until death.

Nara: An ancient sage who was the son of Dharma and Ahimsa.

Narayana: An ancient sage who was one of the two sons of Dharma and Ahimsa. The word also means "Vishnu."

Om: The most sacred word in the Hindu scriptures. Also written as Aum, it is a symbol of God.

Panda: A priest who helps pilgrims in a place of pilgrimage.

Prasad: Consecrated food. Food that has been offered to God.

Puja: Worship.

Glossary

Pujari: A person who performs the worship.

Pundit: A scholar.

Raja-Yoga: The Path of Meditation; one of the four fundamental types of spiritual disciplines that lead to the experience of the Ultimate Reality or Divinity.

Rishi: A sage.

Sadhana: Spiritual practice.

Sadhu: A holy man.

Samadhi: A high state of spiritual ecstasy when the meditator mentally communes with God. There are different kinds of samadhi depending upon the various states of mental concentration.

Sannyasa: The final vows of monastic life.

Sannyasi: One who has taken the final vows of monastic life.

Sevashrama: The word literally means a "home of service."

Sevak: Attendant.

Shavda Brahma: The sound Om as Brahman (God).

Sri Sri Chandi: A part of the *Markandeya Purana* describing the various aspects of the Divine Mother.

Sri Sri Ramakrishna Kathamrita: The name of a book that literally means "The ambrosia-like words of Sri Sri Ramakrishna."

Swami: A Hindu monk who has taken the final vows of monastic life.

Tanmatras: The elementary constituents of the universe. Tanmatras are extremely subtle.

Tantradharaka: A person who guides a worshipper through an elaborate ritualistic worship, and also prompts him with the holy chants, etc. during the worship.

Tapasya: Spiritual austerities.

Thakur: Lord.

Yogabhrashta Rishi: A spiritual aspirant who made high spiritual progress, either in this life or in some past life, but who fell short of having spiritual enlightenment.

Life in Indian Monasteries

LIST OF ILLUSTRATIONS

(continued)

List of Illustrations (continuation)

V

Varanasi
  Advaita ashrama 65
  Sevashrama 12, 21, 94, 99, 106
Videhananda, Swami 115
Vidyatmananda, Swami 178
Vijnanananda, Swami 20, 79
Vireswarananda, Swami 25, 65, 85, 171, 173
Vishuddhananda, Swami 27, 42, 115, 161, 168, 172, 186
Vishwarupananda, Swami 94
Vishwashrayananda, Swami 52, 171
Viswavedananda, Swami 35
Vivekananda, Swami 1, 4, 5, 15, 43, 53, 78, 108, 122, 159, 164
  disciples of 156
Vividishananda, Swami 173, 180
Vrindaban 1
Vrindaban ashrama 89

Y

Yatiswarananda, Swami 182
Yogabhrashta rishi 153
Yogiswarananda, Swami 105
Yuganayak Vivekananda 52

Z

Zushi, Japan 133

Swami Bhaskarananda, born in November 1930, and educated in India, joined the Ramakrishna Order as a monk in January 1958. He was attached to the Headquarters of the Order at Belur (near Calcutta) for 12 years before being posted to Seattle in 1974. He has been President of the Vedanta Society

of Western Washington in Seattle since 1980. He is also the spiritual head of the Vedanta Society in Hawaii and the Vedanta Society in Vancouver (Canada). On invitation, the Swami has traveled extensively in the United States, Canada, Brazil, Argentina, Uruguay, England, France, Japan, Iceland, and the Netherlands, giving talks on Hinduism and other spiritual topics. He has also visited China, Russia, New Zealand and Australia. He is a founding member and past President of the Interfaith Council of Washington State and is currently an Interfaith Partner in the Church Council of Greater Seattle. The Swami is the author of the books *The Essentials of Hinduism* and *Meditation, Mind and Patanjali's Yoga* and is the founder and editor-in-chief of the quarterly journal *Global Vedanta*.

Other Titles by Swami Bhaskarananda

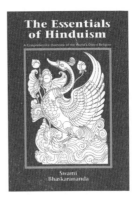

Meditation, Mind and Patanjali's Yoga

A Practical Guide to Spiritual Growth for Everyone

"I have gone through Swami Bhaskarananda's book, *Meditation, Mind and Patanjali's Yoga.* The manuscript is wonderful. Very clear and very very well presented. I thoroughly enjoyed it. I myself would buy it and would recommend it to my students too."

—Prof. John Grimes
Dept. of Religious Studies
Michigan State University

253 pages • paperback • illustrated, with glossary, index, appendices, & suggested reading. Price: $14.50 • ISBN 1-884852-03-3

The Essentials of Hinduism

Acclaimed by many to be the best book on Hinduism…

"I have never been able to find such a helpful work. I shall recommend it enthusiastically for use by our college students."

—Rev. James Roberts
Professor of Religious Studies
Vancouver Community College
Vancouver, British Columbia, Canada

252 pages • paperback • illustrated, with glossary, index, appendices, & suggested reading. Price: $14.50 • ISBN 1-884852-04-1

Ordering information

Vedanta Society Bookshop
2716 Broadway Ave. E
Seattle, WA 98102-3909
Phone: (206) 323-1228
Fax: (206) 329-1791
Email: bookshop@vedanta-seattle.org
Web: www.vedanta-seattle.org

$14.50 each book (add 8.8% sales tax within Washington State). Shipping and handling (US only): Priority mail $4.00; Media mail $1.50. Two or more books shipped without charge. Call or write for international shipping. VISA, MASTERCARD or DISCOVER credit cards accepted.